The ABC Guide to Mindfulness

A teach-yourself course on getting more from life through kindly awareness

By Tim Segaller

Acknowledgements

I'd like to thank some very fine people for the various ways in which they have helped make this book possible. So, heartfelt thanks to all the following people...

....starting with the Buddhists (as that's where mindfulness started!) – Dr Paramabandhu Groves, for his characteristically concise and to-the-point foreword, for being my first formal mindfulness teacher through his excellent mindfulness-based cognitive therapy (MBCT) course at the London Buddhist Centre (LBC), and for his friendship and professional guidance; Maitreyabandhu, another superb teacher at the LBC, who was largely responsible for enticing me to work at the LBC some years ago, also for his friendship and mentorship; and all the other excellent teachers of mindfulness and meditation that I encountered during those years, and the very good friends I made along the way.

....staying with Buddhists, but segueing into my family – my late paternal grandfather, Denis Segaller, a rather extraordinary man who emigrated to Thailand before I was born and converted to Buddhism. I met him twice, both times in Thailand, once aged 8 and the other at 28. Hearing him talk about Buddhism and meditation on my second visit left its mark: though I didn't pursue things further at the time, I stored it away in my memory as one way to achieve the equanimity that so often had eluded me.

....the rest of my family – particularly my wonderfully kind, patient and good-humoured Mum and Dad – for their love and support (of many kinds!)

....my friends throughout my life, also for their love, support and encouragement.

... my therapist, not least for the amazing work she has done with me over the years, but more specifically, it's thanks to her that I got into mindfulness in the first place. She regularly encouraged me to take up meditation to support the therapeutic work. I didn't really take her seriously at first, but eventually I booked myself onto a meditation retreat, and I haven't looked back since.

....Michele Grant, co-founder and fellow director of our coaching and mindfulness social enterprise Rising Minds, for encouraging me to write this book in the first place, and for her very helpful comments on the first draft.

....Mahbub Ahmed, for his delightful illustrations, that capture so beautifully some of the key points of the text.

....Barbara Vesey, Maggie Berney, and my Dad for their laser-sharp proofreading and editing (and for the amusing notes in the margin!)

...Sarah Smith, for the manuscript format and layout.

....Michelle Abrahall, for the striking front-cover design.

...Zoe Dewar and Jane Brant, for taking this book through to its final production and publishing stages on Amazon and CreateSpace.

Thank you again, to all. May you all be well and happy.

Disclaimer

Although the author and publisher have made every effort to ensure that the information in this book was correct at press time, the author and publisher do not assume and hereby disclaim any liability to any party for any loss, damage, or disruption caused by errors or omissions, whether such errors or omissions result from negligence, accident or any other cause.

Contents

Foreword

I first came across Jon Kabat-Zinn's use of mindfulness to help with chronic pain and stress on a visit to Toronto in 1993. At that time his work was not widely known in the UK, but was already becoming popular in North America. As a psychiatrist working in the National Health Service and a meditation teacher at the London Buddhist Centre, I was particularly interested later to hear about the adaptation of his work in the UK and Canada for recurrent depression. Randomised controlled trials showed that mindfulness-based cognitive therapy (MBCT) for depression was effective for preventing relapse in people with three or more episodes of depression. Seeing the potential value of this work, in 2004 I decided to run a course at the London Buddhist Centre. I was surprised on two fronts. Firstly, the demand. Even though I ran a large course it was fully booked two months in advance. Secondly, teaching the course, I was impressed by the benefit that I saw people gaining, especially those who applied themselves to the mindfulness practices.

The following year, I adapted the MBCT course for addiction (as that is my specialty), and started teaching mindfulness-based relapse prevention (MBRP), later to be called mindfulness-based addiction recovery (MBAR). Over the last decade there has been an exponential growth of interest in mindfulness, with studies exploring its use in a wide range of conditions. As well as depression, pain, stress and addiction, these include anxiety, eating disorders, psychosis and attention deficit hyperactivity disorder (ADHD). Although much of this work is still preliminary, there is particularly strong evidence for the effectiveness of mindfulness in depression and anxiety – two common and frequently disabling problems.

Given the demand for the mindfulness courses and the benefits they were giving, we decided at the London Buddhist Centre to create a dedicated space in which we could teach the mindfulness-based approaches and to appoint a manager to oversee the work. We called the project 'Breathing Space' and Tim was appointed as our first manager. One of the things that struck me from the feedback of participants on our courses was the comment that they had been given a toolkit that they could apply to help them with their mood. This is something I really like about mindfulness – it's very practical.

The ABC Guide to Mindfulness elegantly and concisely describes these tools. They are simple, but profound, and can– as I have witnessed – be life-changing. The clear ABC structure is like three successive layers of practice that build on each other to help you work creatively with your mind. Tim's own experience of teaching mindfulness and applying it to his own life shines out in the pages. In particular, drawing on his experience as a coach and blending in elements from positive psychology and Acceptance and Commitment Therapy (ACT), he has expanded the third stage, making wise choices, beyond what is usually found in a mindfulness course. The result is a refreshingly slim, essentialised guide to help you make the most of mindfulness to overcome emotional difficulties and to lead a rich and fulfilling life.

Dr Paramabanhdu Groves
Consultant Psychiatrist and Clinical Director of Breathing Space at the London Buddhist Centre

About the author

Tim Segaller is a coach, trainer and facilitator; specialist in the field of psychological resilience, and a pioneer of the integration of mindfulness and coaching techniques for professional and personal development.

He is Co-Founder and Director of Rising Minds, a social enterprise helping people both in organisations and in the community to uncover their natural energy, clarity and resolve to thrive in their lives and work.

In businesses and organisations Tim specialises in helping leaders and teams develop in three key areas:

- **Mental resilience**: developing a steady mind in the face of stressful demands — for better focus, clearer thinking, and natural productivity

- **Authentic leadership**: reconnecting with personal and natural leadership capabilities, and true sources of inspiration and enjoyment at work

- **Building strong relationships**: developing a 'co-active' leadership and communication style that makes it easier to lead others and support their development

Through social projects for people in the community, and through 1-1 coaching work, Tim supports people from many walks of life to make big changes and decisions in their personal or professional lives, or simply to feel better in themselves.

Through pioneering the integration of coaching and mindfulness techniques, Tim has a distinctive working style that pays attention to the full spectrum of his clients' experience – the head and heart; and the mind and body. His clients particularly appreciate his balance between calm, encouraging support; and structured, rigorous challenge – enabling them to gain quick insights, break through obstacles and achieve sustainable change.

Tim is a Professional Certified Coach with the International Coach Federation (ICF) – the leading worldwide professional coaching body and holds a Diploma in Business and Executive Coaching from Coaching Development. He's also an accredited mindfulness trainer and workplace mediator.

Prior to interpersonal work, Tim's background was in communications and project management in the private and third sectors, after gaining a First-Class degree in Classics from Oxford University. Having discovered personally the powerful positive effects of mindfulness, he became the first manager of the London Buddhist Centre's secular mindfulness programme, Breathing Space.

Outside working life, Tim has a creative practice including artwork, filmmaking and writing, including a multimedia project celebrating some of his closest friends (friendsintheframe.com)

For more information and to get in touch with Tim, go to: risingminds.org.uk.

Introduction

This book is a very practical guide to mindfulness, which is about living with more awareness – and more kindness to yourself and others – so that you feel better in yourself and can get the most out of life.

Before I set out what this book covers and how to use it, just a few words about me for some context. I took up mindfulness practice ten years ago at a difficult time in my life. I had been experiencing a lot of mental suffering. Several people – professionally and personally – encouraged me to start meditating as a way of supporting my wellbeing and a healthier sense of myself. Somehow, I knew exactly what they meant, even though I hadn't even yet tried meditation. As someone with a tendency towards getting stressed and uptight, and striving too hard for things, I knew I needed something that could help ground me and hold a bigger perspective on things. I've found that mindfulness practice does just this: it helps me to feel calmer, more grounded and happier in myself.

Over the past decade I've studied and practised mindfulness in a number of different ways – on mindfulness courses, workshops and retreats, and reading some of the plethora of mindfulness books on the market. Together, these have helped me to transform my experience of myself and the world around me – so much so that I wanted to pass on to others what I'd found so invaluable myself. So six years ago I decided to start teaching mindfulness myself. Since then I've taught hundreds of people the key things I've learned, and I hope it would be true to say that they too have noticed significant improvements in their wellbeing and sense of themselves.

As a former copywriter and editor, I also happen to enjoy the process of integrating lots of information, techniques and theory from wide-ranging sources, and then simplifying all of this into concise, straightforward and accessible material. And that's what I've aimed to do in this book. So my hope and belief is that in this slim volume you will find all the tools and theory that you need to start making mindfulness a part of your life, just as I have done in mine.

The book takes you through an experiential learning process over at least six weeks – which you can either do on your own, or with tailored 1-1 coaching with me It's best not to read it straight through, however much you are enjoying it!

Let's define mindfulness as 'paying attention, on purpose, in the present moment'. In other words, it's about developing *awareness* of what's going on in and around you. And with 'attention' and 'awareness', that's not about observing things in a cold, clinical way – rather it's about noticing and understanding your experience with gentleness and kindness.

When you learn mindfulness in this way, you develop some simple but powerful ways to work more effectively with your own mind. These have been shown in lots of studies to help people enjoy life more – to feel emotionally stronger and more naturally positive, and better able to deal with stresses and problems. As said above, I can testify from personal experience to the truth of this.

You'll be learning and practising a range of skills to pay more attention to your present-moment experience – your thoughts, emotions, and body sensations. These include meditations, simple physical movements, and written exercises and reflections.

The book is structured around a simple ABC model, which will become clearer as you go through the chapters. But to give you a sneak preview, this is what the ABC stands for:

A. Awareness: of what is happening in your present-moment experience.

B. Being with your experience: cultivating an attitude of kindly acceptance to yourself – your thoughts and emotions – and the world around you.

C. Choosing wise responses to your experience, by *responding* wisely instead of *reacting* automatically.

I came across this ABC on the very first mindfulness course I attended at the London Buddhist Centre. It was included as a relatively short section in the handout for one of the later sessions of the course. Apparently, a participant on a previous course had come up with it as a useful mnemonic for themselves. Later, when devising my own first mindfulness course, I was reviewing my course notes, and the ABC struck me as a beautifully simple and complete way of capturing the essence and practice of mindfulness. It shows that mindfulness is not just a set of techniques, skills and attitudes, but also a *process* that one can consciously take oneself through. There is a kind of a narrative flow to it – a sense of the general positive direction one can take when practising mindfulness. So I have adopted the ABC for the structure of this book and the mindfulness journey you are about to embark on.

To support you along this journey, you are encouraged to do some practice every day. The exercises for each chapter are shown at the end of that chapter. They include some guided meditations. You can access the accompanying audio files (to stream or download) at: risingminds.org.uk/mindfulness

It's recommended that you spend at least a week on the daily home practice for each chapter before you move on to the next chapter. That means that the whole course will take you at least six weeks to complete.

Learning mindfulness can be extremely enjoyable – and it can open up a wholly different way of being, leading to a greater sense of wellbeing and control of your life and emotions. But like any skill, it takes time and effort to learn. This being so, you are encouraged to commit as much of yourself as you can to doing the home practice – ideally every day if you can. You will be challenging old patterns of your mind, and for those to loosen and shift, repeated practice is the key.

However, it's also really important that you adopt – as best you can – a kind and gentle approach towards yourself in relation to doing the home practice. So if you do miss a day, don't give yourself a hard time, as that will be counterproductive. Instead, just see if you can renew a commitment to yourself to pick up the practice again. There are some tips in Chapter 2 about how to set things up best for yourself to encourage regular practice.

Good luck on your mindfulness journey!

Tim Segaller, London 2018

Chapter 1
Introducing mindfulness

The bad news: life can be difficult

First, let's get the bad news out of the way: life can be difficult. Of course, it can also be wonderful and fulfilling. But it can be difficult – sometimes very difficult. You know this already. Everyone is prone to physical and mental suffering. Sickness and illness cause the body to suffer. Unpleasant emotions – like anger, sadness, or frustration – cause the mind to suffer. Those emotions come about due to some simple truths about the human experience of life:

- *You don't always get what you want*: be that a certain job or relationship, a pay rise, enough time to yourself, or that sports car or designer dress you've been coveting. The list could go on and on ...

- *You can't avoid everything you don't want*: whether that's getting a cold, doing the daily commute, technology not working properly, someone being rude to you. Again, the examples are infinite ...

- *Some things change that you may wish could stay the same*: like your body deteriorating as you age, relationships or jobs coming to an end, or good weather turning bad. You can probably think of your own examples.

- *Some things stay the same that you may wish could change*: particularly, certain habits in yourself or other people.

All these 'problems' are part and parcel of being human, and you can't avoid them completely. If you think you can, you are either a) somewhat deluded, or b) not a human being!

You can sometimes make things worse for yourself

So there are inevitable problems and difficulties in life. However, how your mind reacts to these 'original' problems can dramatically affect your quality of life. Often you may make things worse for yourself without realising you are doing so. Let's explain how this happens.

How the mind has evolved to solve problems through 'autopilot'

The starting point is a basic understanding of how the human mind has evolved to be a highly effective problem-solving machine. In humanity's prehistoric past, the mind developed in this way in order to avoid the perils of predators and a hostile environment. In order to survive, the mind needed to perceive danger and to figure out how to protect against it. This is what's known as the 'fight/flight/freeze' response to danger: when faced with a life-threatening situation, early humans needed either to fight off the enemy, run away from it, or become invisible. They needed to find one of these solutions very quickly, as the threat was instant and total. As a result the mind developed an *'autopilot mode'* that can take in a lot of data quickly through the senses, calculate what it means, and come up with a solution – all in a split second.

Autopilot is very useful in many areas of life

While modern human beings don't often need to defend against life-threatening danger, the autopilot mode is very much in operation. And it's still extremely useful in many areas of life. It allows routine tasks to be carried out without having to 'solve the problem' each time. Technically speaking, it creates habits in order to extend 'working memory capacity'. It's what makes multi-tasking possible. For example, think about getting dressed this morning: presumably you didn't have to work out *how* to put your clothes on. And you probably were thinking about all sorts of other things while you were getting dressed. That's because you have learned a habit for getting dressed – just as you have learned habits for countless activities that you do without having to work out consciously each time how to do them. Imagine how complicated life would be without this habit-making ability.

But autopilot is not so helpful when it comes to emotions

All well and good so far. However, problems can start to arise when this autopilot mode is allowed to get too involved in every aspect of life. In particular, it can be very unhelpful when it takes over the job of managing one's mood. Here's what can happen ...

Everyone feels unpleasant emotions at times – like sadness, anxiety, or irritability. When autopilot first notices the presence of an unpleasant emotion, it automatically detects it as a 'problem' and steps in to try and fix things. However, this simply doesn't work because emotions – even the most difficult ones – are not in fact 'problems' to be fixed, they are a normal feature of human existence. In fact, emotions are carriers of vital information, and sometimes it's better to allow them simply to be felt, even if they are not pleasant.

There will be more about this later in the book.

The link between thoughts and moods

Not only does autopilot not work in 'fixing' difficult problems, it can often make things much worse. The reason for this lies in the strong link between thoughts and moods. It's been known for several decades that thoughts can drive moods. This discovery is the fundamental basis of Cognitive Behavioural Therapy, which helps alleviate low mood by enabling people to become aware of the nature of their habitual thoughts, and start to challenge and change them.

What's more interesting is that this process works in reverse as well: moods can drive thoughts. So, one morning you might wake up feeling a bit low, or anxious, or irritable. It may even only be a slight feeling. As you notice this is how you feel, you may then have a whole range of 'negative' thoughts in response, which tend to have one or more of three main features:

1) Self-attacking – e.g. 'I am feeling like this because there is something wrong with me.'

2) Blaming others – 'This is my boss's fault for making me work too hard.'

3) Comparing against some ideal version of how things should be – 'I don't want to feel like this, I want to feel happy. This isn't supposed to be happening.'

The downward spiral

Because thoughts drive moods, all these kinds of 'negative' thoughts are likely to worsen your difficult mood, which then gives rise to more 'negative' thoughts, which can worsen your mood yet further. And so a downward spiral is set up, which can be very hard to get out of.

For example, let's imagine you've got some important and difficult task to complete – perhaps at work or something in your personal life – that you've been putting off for a while. You're concerned that you're not going to be able to do it to your own or others' satisfaction. It's making you feel anxious. You finally decide to attempt it. But you're feeling so uptight about it that you can't think straight, and can't work out how to do it. You start to believe that you're not up to the job. Having that thought makes you feel even more anxious, and then you may start to believe that this means you're not going to be able to do other challenging things in the future. That thought leads to an even worse mood, in turn leading to even more catastrophic thoughts. And so the downward spiral spins ever deeper …

This process can be made even worse by the role that memory plays: when things get difficult, there is a tendency to remember all the times that those emotions have been felt, and this just reinforces the low mood.

All of this is happening at an unconscious, automatic level. That's because autopilot has been left unchecked to create a whole set of 'mental habits' – like grooves in the mind – that lead to stress, low mood, exhaustion or just general unhappiness. These mental habits are perhaps the most significant contributory factor in cases of depression and anxiety.

At a physiological level, what's happening is that autopilot has allowed the 'fight/flight/freeze' response to kick in – the body gets braced for dealing with life-threatening danger, when in fact there isn't any such danger. In the process a lot of energy gets sapped from the body – energy that in fact could be preserved. Conversely, when this vital life energy is preserved, it allows for a more abiding sense of wellbeing and ease most of the time.

So the 'problem' here is not the original unpleasant emotion, but the reaction to it. It's the very attempt to free yourself from that emotion that is making it worse. Pushing too hard at a problem uses up a lot of energy, and you're left drained and feeling defeated. And it's all because you have allowed your autopilot mode to have way too much power.

Autopilot leading to a downward spiral of emotions

The good news: there is another way

So now for the good news: there is another way to relate to life's inevitable problems and to the difficult emotions everyone experiences at times. You can learn how to go against the tide of old habitual and unhelpful tendencies of the mind. You can learn to surf the ups and downs of life – enabling you to be more consistently and reliably happy and content, and better able to fulfil your potential.

'Being' instead of 'doing'

So how do you do this? The answer is simple: by engaging a different mode of your mind. Autopilot always wants to fix things and solve problems. It's the 'doing' mode of the mind – it's like your mind's handyman! As explained above, it simply doesn't work when it comes to the job of managing your mood and emotions. It has volunteered for the wrong job.

The alternative mode of the mind you can engage is what can be called the 'being' mode. Everyone has the capacity to use it – but it is often under-developed. It's the part of your mind that can:

- simply observe and sense, in a gentle and patient way, how things are *in this moment*, letting them be as they actually are rather than needing to fix or change anything

- understand that everything in your experience is constantly changing

- step back from things, give them some space and allow them to change in their own natural way.

'Approach' instead of 'avoid'

Another way of describing this 'being' mode of the mind is 'approach' mode. It's able to take a real interest in what is actually going on in your experience, including difficult things. This is the opposite of 'avoidance', which is what often happens in the 'doing' mode. Autopilot tries to fix things instantly, without taking the time and space needed to assess what is actually happening in a situation. And this is actually a form of avoidance: rather than facing a difficulty head on, it tries to get round it by coming up with a quick fix. This unhelpful avoidance mode is very common among people who have perfectionist tendencies: the compelling need to avoid failure means that they stop taking risks, or looking at things differently. There is often an accompanying sense of being trapped. If you are one of these people (and it's a very common tendency), you will probably recognise yourself.

You can develop this alternative approach through mindfulness

There's more good news: it is possible to consciously train and develop this 'being' mode of your mind. The training used to do this is called ... **mindfulness**.

The mindful way

Let's start with a short definition: mindfulness is a way of training your mind to pay attention – without judgement – in the present moment to your experience in your body and mind.

So when you train in mindfulness, you learn to notice what is actually going on inside and around you. And importantly, you learn to notice things without judging them as good or bad, or trying to change them instantly – even if you don't like them. You simply notice them, give them space to be as they are, and stay open to how they might change.

As you will see throughout this book, in order to be able to develop this ability to notice things, it really helps if you can also do so with an attitude of kindness, gentleness and patience.

So mindfulness is noticing what you notice, and doing so gently and kindly. It's about sometimes just being rather than always doing.

Mindfulness has its roots in ancient practices. It has been adopted in the secular West by health services, businesses and organisations as a training to promote personal wellbeing and effectiveness. It still uses the same original basic tools and techniques that have been practised successfully for thousands of years. These are 'awareness' techniques: some of them practised formally through simple meditations, and others practised more informally throughout your everyday life. It's these techniques that you will learn on this mindfulness training programme.

The ABC of mindfulness

Mindfulness can be broken down into a simple ABC process, which this book is structured around.

A. You start by developing **Awareness** of what is happening in your experience, with kindness and patience. This is done initially through meditation, mindful exercises, and being mindful of other activities during the day, such as walking or eating.

B. Next, you learn to **Be with your experience**. You start by noticing how your experiences are created by the interlinking patterns of your thoughts and moods. You do this by watching your thoughts more carefully. Next, you can learn to cultivate an attitude of acceptance towards difficult experiences, instead of pushing them away.

C. Finally, you can **Choose wise responses** to your experience.

Having given your mind and body more time and space to become aware and be with your experience, you allow the most helpful decisions and choices to emerge. The key here is *responding* wisely instead of *reacting* automatically.

Of course, it's worth saying that life is not really linear, nor is the way we learn, so it's not that you will first totally master the A of 'Awareness' before moving on to the B of 'Being with', mastering that, and then going on to the C of 'Choosing wise responses'. It's more of an iterative process – so you will be learning to keep coming back to Awareness again and again, and then moving through the B and the C as many times as you need to, before coming back to Awareness yet again. As you will hopefully find, it's going to be about allowing this process to become second nature – a new way of being – rather than something that you have to consciously take yourself through.

Autopilot v Mindfulness

The difference between the two modes of mind – autopilot (or doing, or avoid mode) and mindfulness (or being, or approach mode) can be seen in the diagram on the next page. It shows what happens in each mode when a problem or difficult emotion arises.

What's the point of mindfulness?

Mindfulness training helps you get out of the 'doing' mode of autopilot when what's needed is more of a 'being' mode. This enables you to deal more effectively with the emotional challenges of life. This is backed up by a huge body of clinical research, which shows that mindfulness training is highly effective in alleviating stress, anxiety, depression and chronic pain and illness. Specific benefits include:

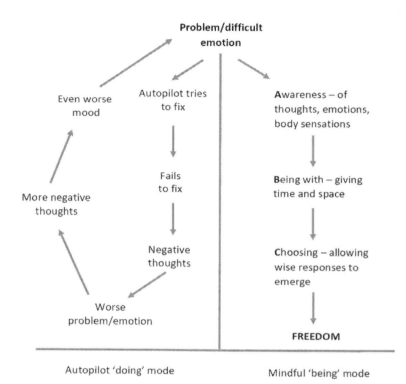

Problem/difficult emotion

Even worse mood

Autopilot tries to fix

Awareness – of thoughts, emotions, body sensations

Fails to fix

Being with – giving time and space

More negative thoughts

Negative thoughts

Choosing – allowing wise responses to emerge

Worse problem/emotion

FREEDOM

Autopilot 'doing' mode

Mindful 'being' mode

- *Less stress* – and more resilience as you learn better responses to difficult situations, and to turn off the damaging 'fight/flight/freeze' response in your body more of the time.

- *Clearer mind* – increased attention, concentration and memory enable you to do things better and faster.

- *Emotional intelligence* – as you become aware of what's going on for you and others, you're better able to communicate assertively while kindly, and so build healthier relationships.

- *Creativity* – and innovative thinking, due to an ability to hold a wider perspective and think 'outside the box'.

- *Decision-making* – and problem-solving skills, particularly at times of high pressure, as your mind sifts through lots of data more intuitively and efficiently.

- *Healthy body* – an enhanced ability to relax in your mind and body leads to a stronger immune system and alleviates problems like hypertension, heart disease and chronic pain.

- *More enjoyment* – mindfulness isn't only about alleviating problems, it's also about finding out what really makes you tick, so that you can do more of what gives you a sense of pleasure and fulfilment.

Mindfulness and the brain

People who regularly practise mindfulness usually know from their own experience how it benefits them. But recent research in neuroscience has been backing up this subjective evidence. Let's put some of these findings into some context about how the brain works.

The brain transmits information between cells through chemical neurotransmitters. Repeated exchange of information builds up pathways and networks, which is what makes humans creatures of habit. The brain develops only through its responses to experiences – the data that comes to it through the senses. This means that the brain can be shaped and changed by what you give your attention to('neuroplasticity').

As a result it's possible to unlearn old habits and replace them with new ones. This is where mindfulness training is so helpful — it teaches you how to pay attention. You can then choose what to pay attention to.

One helpful way of showing how mindfulness can improve brain functioning is in the context of the human 'three-part brain'.

1) The reptilian brain

Humans share this brain part with birds and reptiles. It's responsible for basic functions like breathing and heart rate. It's the autopilot part of the brain that allows you to do routine tasks. Mindfulness training can help you to embed useful routines — e.g. doing regular exercise. By making these automatic, more energy is freed up for more complex work and thinking.

2) The limbic system (or mammalian brain)

Humans share this brain part with mammals. It's responsible for regulating emotions. So, like the reptile brain, it doesn't deal in logic — it tends to react automatically to things. This is to do with the way humans have evolved to protect against threats: early humans needed something to provoke a quick response. This is the role that 'survival' emotions like fear and anger play.

Interestingly, the brain can't actually distinguish between a real threat to your life (a wild animal chasing after you) and a 'superficial' threat (someone being rude to you, or an urgent deadline). This has major consequences for your wellbeing and quality of life.

So, whenever you perceive a threat – real or superficial – your limbic system gets activated, often leading to a chain of events in the brain, nervous system and body. In the brain, a part called the amygdala takes over, overriding logical thinking. It then switches on the sympathetic nervous system, which in turn can trigger the 'fight, flight or freeze' response. This causes blood and energy to rush to the muscles, and stress hormones to be released. If this happens too often, it can be damaging to organs and the immune system. That's because the parasympathetic nervous system – which is responsible for growth, healing and maintenance – gets switched off. Also, excess stress hormones can injure or kill brain cells, and cause burn-out.

Mindfulness can help regulate the limbic system. It helps you to become more aware of your emotional triggers, and then to put more space between the emotion and your automatic reaction to it. You still have an initial emotional reaction to threats, but you can limit the potentially damaging effect it has on your moods and body.

3) The neocortex (or rational brain)

The neocortex is found only in primates and is the most sophisticated part of the brain. It's responsible for advance planning, abstract thought and imagination. By managing your reptilian brain and limbic system more effectively through mindfulness practice, as described above, more energy is freed up for the neocortex to process information, think rationally and make wise choices. Mindfulness can also help you regulate the energy that's required for the neocortex. It does this by detecting in the first place that a rest is needed, and also by providing simple techniques for how to have a good rest – even if that's only quite short.

How to approach this programme

Mindfulness training involves challenging and changing some old, automatic patterns of mind. This will take some time and effort. So you are invited to adopt an attitude of kindness towards yourself – encouraging yourself, and being as patient and gentle with yourself as you can. It's recommended to do some 'home practice' every day. The practice will involve formal meditation, mindful movement exercises, and some other simple daily activities. It's up to you how much of this you do. Of course, it's great if you can do as much of the home practice as you can: the more you put in, the more you'll get out. Try to do a bit every day, however much you can manage.

For this chapter, you will be invited to start practising the 'waking up to yourself' meditation, which will help you develop awareness in the present moment – the foundation of mindfulness. Details of how to access the audio guided meditation are provided at the end of this chapter.

Some initial tips about mindfulness practice

It's best not to overload you at this early stage with too much information about mindfulness and meditation practice. That's because mindfulness is best understood through practising it, not just reading about it. You've got plenty of information to absorb already in this chapter – and it's best to discover *for yourself* the insights and benefits that mindfulness practice offers. So it's best to wait until the next chapter for more detailed guidance about meditation – what it is, what it isn't, and how best to approach it. But for now, here are just a few things worth noting as you start out:

- **The main thing you are doing is learning to notice things** – particularly in your body: so in the first meditation you will be practising (the 'waking up to yourself' meditation), simply follow the instructions about where to focus your attention. Your mind will keep wandering off – that's fine, it's just what the mind does. You can just accept this and then repeatedly bring back your attention to the body or the breath – with kindness, gentleness and patience. Each time you do this you are strengthening your mindfulness 'muscle'.

- **You are not supposed to be clearing your mind of all thoughts** (which is actually impossible anyway): instead you are starting to become more familiar with the way your mind works and how generally scattered it probably is.

- **You cannot get meditation wrong**: there is no particular state of mind you are supposed to 'achieve': achievement is what the 'doing' mode of the mind wants … but remember: you are learning to open up a different 'being' mode. So you can just let go of any expectations of what *should* be happening in the meditation, and simply notice what is *actually* happening, particularly in your body.

- **Relaxation may or may not happen**: Of course if you are feeling stressed or restless it's natural to want to relax. But if you try to relax, it probably won't happen. Instead you are simply learning to pay attention to your experience. You may find that by doing so, you *naturally* relax. If so, that's great and you can enjoy it. But if it doesn't happen, it does not mean you have failed to do the meditation correctly. **This cannot be over-emphasised!**

Short summary of this chapter

Life contains some problems that simply can't be avoided. But often you may make things worse for yourself by how you react to the original problem. This can be explained by how the mind has evolved to have an 'autopilot' mode, which immediately tries to solve problems. 'Autopilot' is very useful in carrying out routine tasks – you don't have to work out how to do them every time. But it's not so helpful when you experience a difficult emotion like sadness or anxiety, or irritability. It tries to 'fix' it, but it can't do so – because emotions don't need to be 'fixed', they are a normal feature of human existence.

The very failure of autopilot to fix things can then make you feel worse, because it can lead to negative and self-attacking thoughts about why you shouldn't be feeling the way you are. And then, because thoughts and moods are so closely linked, your mood may get worse, giving rise to more negative thoughts, then your mood gets even worse ... and so you find yourself in a downward spiral. This whole process happens at an unconscious level – you don't mean to do this to yourself. You have simply created a 'mental habit' of thinking and feeling in this way. And it's all because autopilot mode has been allowed to have way too much power.

There is another way to relate to problems and difficult emotions. By practising mindfulness, you learn to simply notice things, without judging them as good or bad, or trying to instantly change them – even if you don't like them. The training involves very simple 'awareness' techniques, including formal meditations, and other informal activities throughout your day.

This book is structured around a simple ABC of Mindfulness:

<u>A</u>wareness – of what is happening in your experience

<u>B</u>eing with your experience – accepting what is already there and what cannot be fixed immediately

<u>C</u>hoosing wise responses – instead of *reacting* automatically, allowing the most helpful actions and choices to emerge

Home practice before the next chapter

To stream or download the audio guided meditations listed below, go to: risingminds.org.uk/mindfulness

1. 'Waking up to yourself' meditation: Follow the instructions on the audio guided meditation. Do this every day, or as close to this as you can manage.

2. Mindful minute: Several times a day, stop what you're doing for 30 seconds or so. With your eyes open or closed, notice your body, and notice what you can see, hear, smell, taste or touch. Allow all of these things to merge into a general awareness of what's going on right now in and around you. You can do this on your own, or by listening to the 'mindful minute' on the audio (when appropriate).

3. Do a routine activity 'mindfully': Pick a routine activity that you do every day – for example, brushing your teeth, or making a cup of tea. Instead of doing it on 'autopilot' as normally happens, try and get into more of a 'being' mode by bringing awareness to the physical sensations of the movements your body makes. Notice anything else coming into you through your senses: sounds, textures, light and colour, smells and so on. Bring curiosity and interest to how this routine activity feels different each time you do it, when

you pay this special kind of attention.

4. Do something different: Sit in a different chair from the one you usually do – at home, at work, or wherever else you go frequently. What does it feel like? What do you notice when you change something around like this?

Journaling

It can be helpful to keep a simple journal of what you are noticing as you start to practise mindfulness. For this chapter, jot down whatever feels relevant to you as you do the home practice. If you get stuck about what to write, here are a few questions to prompt reflection:

- *How much time do you normally spend in 'doing' mode?*
- *What happens when you focus your attention on one part of your body, or your breath? How easy is it?*
- *What's different about doing a routine activity when you notice what it feels like in your body?*

Chapter 2
The A of the ABC: Awareness

The last chapter introduced the concept of mindfulness as a way of training the mind to pay attention in the present moment. This chapter has more about what mindfulness is, and focuses on the A of the ABC - Awareness. It also looks in greater depth at meditation, which is the primary tool for developing mindfulness. And it describes in more detail two key practices for you to do at home using the audio guided meditations.

More about mindfulness

Training the mind to pay attention ... *and* to pay attention to your attention

Mindfulness firstly describes a way of training the mind. As explained in Chapter 1, this training is about activating a 'being' mode, which is able to stand back from situations and give them more space and time. It's in contrast to the 'doing' mode of autopilot, which is dominant most of the time and can lead into difficulties when you are faced with certain problems, particularly with your emotions.

The way you train your mind to get into this 'being' mode is by paying attention to what's going on in your present-moment physical experience, particularly in your body. So at the simplest level, mindfulness means paying attention.

But very importantly, mindfulness is also about learning to notice when your attention has wandered. And then, when this happens, it's about avoiding giving yourself a hard time that your mind has wandered – i.e. being kind to yourself. So it could be said that mindfulness also involves paying attention to your attention! The more you do this, the more you learn how to pay attention in the first place. Later in this chapter there will be more about what this means and how to practise it both in formal meditation and in other informal activities.

A different way of being

As well as being a method for training the mind, mindfulness also describes the result of that training – which is a very different way of being from how many people normally tend to go through life. Fundamentally, it's about being able to see things *as they really are*, rather than how you might fear or want them to be. And not only seeing things as they really are, but also allowing them to be that way – without always trying to change them straight away. As a result, mindfulness practice enables you to *open up the broadest perspectives* on yourself, other people, and the situations you find yourself in. Most people who practise mindfulness find that these broader perspectives naturally include a strong element of kindness and patience. There will be more on all of these points later in the book – this is just a taster of what to expect in what lies ahead.

The primary mindfulness tool: meditation

Meditation is the main tool you can use to train yourself to become more mindful. It's not the only tool – and there will be more throughout this book about how you can incorporate mindfulness into everything that you do. But for now, the focus will be on meditation.

What meditation is

There are countless forms of meditation from a wide array of traditions, developed over thousands of years. This is not the place to detail those. However, what most of them have in common is an emphasis on developing your ability to *focus on one thing at a time and to notice when you have stopped doing so*. And this is exactly what mindfulness practice is about. Its ultimate aim is to develop your overall awareness – and it uses concentration as the main tool.

It's worth mentioning here how Western science has only recently discovered something that meditators have known for millennia: *the process of observation changes the things that are being observed*. For example, in certain conditions when you look at an electron, it's a particle; in other conditions, it's a wave. The same is true of observing the mind, which is ultimately just a set of 'events'. As self- reflective beings, humans actually participate in and affect those events when they are observed. So meditation is 'participatory observation' – what you are looking at responds to being looked at. That's what you'll be finding out as you practise mindfulness.

What meditation isn't

It's helpful to dispel a few myths about what meditation is *not*:

- *Emptying your mind:* which is actually impossible to do anyway. Instead you are learning to become more familiar with what is actually going on in your mind.

- *Having no thoughts:* again, this is an impossible goal. Rather, the aim here is to see what thoughts you actually do have. And as you will see later, it's about learning to have more 'distance' from your thoughts so that they don't have such a strong hold over you.

- *A harsh discipline that requires you to be very tough with yourself:* while it's true that it does take some effort and self-discipline to learn mindfulness skills and techniques, it's also vital to approach this learning process with a sense of kindness towards yourself. Like any new skill, mindfulness takes some time and dedication to master, and so it's going to be much easier to learn if you can go about this in a steady and patient way.

- *Just about learning how to relax:* as said already, the wider goal of meditation is to become aware of what is going on in your experience. That may or may not lead to relaxation. There's more on this shortly.

- *Sticking your head in the sand:* in fact, when you learn mindfulness, you learn how to face reality head on.

- *Becoming selfishly obsessed with your own experience:* when you learn to meditate, you're not only going to improve your own wellbeing, you will also have a positive impact on others around you, as you will be better at understanding them and empathising with them.

Developing awareness through the 'waking up to yourself' meditation

Now that you have a broad view of what mindfulness meditation is and what it isn't, let's get to practical matters, with detailed guidance on the first core meditation on this course – the **'waking up to yourself' meditation**. To practise this all you need to do is follow the instructions on the audio guided meditation. Hopefully you've already been doing this and are fairly confident about what you are doing and why. However, as you get into the practice more, you may find the following notes and tips helpful.

Posture

You can do this meditation in one of three different positions:

- *lying down* with a cushion supporting your head, and with your legs either straight on the floor, or with your knees bent so that the soles of your feet are flat on the floor.

- *sitting on an upright chair* – with both feet firmly on the floor and your back reasonably straight, either against the back of the chair or slightly away from it. Place your hands on your legs or in your lap, in whatever position feels most comfortable.

- *sitting on meditation cushions* (if you have them) – either astride them with your legs parallel to the cushions, or cross-legged on them. You need to find the right height of cushions for your body. If you want to use meditation cushions, it's probably best to check with an experienced meditation instructor that your set-up is right for you.

Posture for sitting on cushions

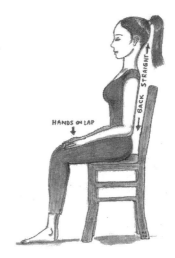

Posture for sitting on a chair

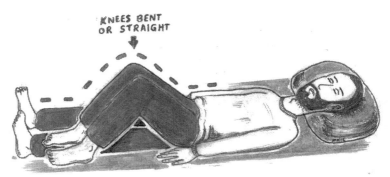

Posture for lying down

With any of the above, you're aiming for a position in which you feel comfortable and relaxed and, at the same time, alert and composed. So if you're sitting on a chair or cushions, the important thing is that your back is straight. Don't pull it *too* straight into a ramrod position – this will create strain. Equally, make sure your head isn't dropping forward, as this can make you feel dull and sleepy.

A good way of checking if you have found the right balance is to imagine a plumb-line dropping down from the crown of your head through your navel and into the cushions or chair. The rest of your body can relax and find a natural balance around this central axis.

Another way to help you get a good posture is to use your breath. You can take a few slightly deeper breaths all the way down into and out of your belly. As you breathe in, you can imagine your breath is travelling along your back, giving you uplift in your back and neck. And as you breathe out, imagine your breath is travelling down your front. This can help you get a sense of being centred and grounded.

The ultimate aim in this meditation is to 'fall awake', not asleep, as you are trying to become more aware of your experience. However, if you are very tired and sleepy, then you may well fall asleep, particularly if you are lying down. Don't worry – it happens. If so, it might be that you just need a good nap, or perhaps you're not getting enough sleep generally – and it could be helpful for you to realise this. But sometimes you might be able to 'go beyond' this sleepiness the more you do this meditation, especially if you choose to sit rather than lie down.

Where and when to meditate

Find a quiet place in your home where you know you won't be disturbed. Ask people not to disturb you for the time you will be meditating. Turn off your mobile phone and anything else that might make a sudden noise. Decide on a regular meditation time each day – e.g. in the morning straight after you get up, or in the evening before you go to bed. Experiment with different times of day. Stay flexible about this.

Doing the practice

The audio guided meditation gives you clear instructions about what to do, so that's not detailed here. But just to summarise the stages of the meditation:

Stage 1: Overall awareness of your body and your breathing
Stage 2: Body scan
Stage 3: Following your breath
Stage 4: Overall body awareness

What's actually happening in this meditation?

In this meditation, you are training yourself in two key related skills:

1) Concentration or 'absorption'

This is your ability to pay attention to your experience. There's nothing that you are meant to be noticing or not noticing – you just notice what you notice. You don't need to try hard to force your concentration, as this will probably be counterproductive. Instead, it's more about allowing the mind to become naturally *absorbed* in the sensations you notice. This is what is meant by *kindly* awareness – rather than forcing things in a hard, tough way, it's better to allow awareness to flourish naturally, over time. It can take some time for this to happen, as thousands of networks in your brain have to rewire and strengthen themselves. Having said that, a bit of effort and willpower is necessary, particularly in these early stages of your mindfulness career, as you build up your mental 'muscle' of attention. The more you practise this, the easier it will become to balance the amount of effort you use to 'power' your concentration.

2) Mindfulness

This is *the ability to notice what is happening to your attention*. So it is your *mindfulness* that will notice when your *concentration* has faded and your mind has wandered off. When this happens, it's not a problem – it's perfectly natural. Each time it happens, you just bring your attention back to your body/breath with kindness and patience. In fact, each time you do it, you are strengthening your overall ability to be mindful.

These two skills – concentration and mindfulness – are intimately linked. And as you practise mindfulness more, you'll see that you can't develop one effectively without the other. If you only developed concentration without mindfulness, you are likely to become too narrowly focused and over-straining. And if you only have mindfulness with no concentration, you may drift off into a sleepy, dreamlike state that may be pleasant in itself, but you won't get one of the key benefits of mindfulness – clearer thinking.

So it's good to aim for a balance of the two: a steady, focused attention on the particular object of meditation (concentration), within a context of a broad, open and kindly awareness of everything that's going on, including where your attention is (mindfulness). As you practise more, you'll get an intuitive sense of this – knowing how and when to switch between the two, and ultimately to blend them together into a balanced state that includes both effort and relaxation.

You might find it helpful to experiment with putting this into practice in the meditation with your breath. So, each time you breathe in, you can imagine you are taking in energy and directing that in a very sharp, focused way towards the object of meditation (e.g. a particular body part). Then as you breathe out, you spread your awareness out more broadly, while still keeping a gentle awareness of the meditation object. There is no rule of thumb for this – see how it works for you.

Should I become relaxed?

As said earlier, the primary aim of this practice is to become aware, and not to make relaxation happen. Having said this, if you notice that you are feeling extremely agitated, stressed or restless, you can use your breathing to help you establish some calm. The best way to do this is to consciously breathe fully in, all the way down into your belly, and then lengthen the outbreath by letting it out slowly through your mouth or nostrils. Do this for as many cycles of the breath as you need, until you feel calmer.

Some people find that counting their breath helps them stay focused. So, you breathe in, and breathe out, and then say silently to yourself 'One', then breathe in and out again and count two, and so on all the way up to ten, and then go back to one. But be prepared for the fact that it won't always work as well as you might want it to. Also, watch out for developing too much of a habit around either controlling or counting your breath in this way. As you practise more and more, you will get to know when this approach is useful.

Why focus attention on the body and the breath?

Most forms of meditation work by having a fixed object for your attention. By focusing on that object, your mind naturally starts to settle down into a clearer, more open awareness of your experience. In this meditation, the object of your attention is your body and your breath. Here is why:

The body
- It is always there as a reliable object for attention. When you practise tuning in to your body, you start to notice how many sensations there are to be felt (including even a lack of sensations).

- The body can help you feel and understand your emotions. Every emotion you experience can be 'located' in the body. In fact, you can usually experience emotions more vividly in the body than in the 'thinking' mind. So the more you get acquainted with your body, the more you understand your own emotions. Later in the book there will be much more on how you can work more effectively with the wide range of different emotions you encounter.

The breath
- Just like the body, the breath is always there as a reliable object for your attention. It was there the moment you were born, and will be there until the moment you die.

- The breath breathes itself. You don't have to make it happen, or manipulate it. Instead you can tune in to it and simply let yourself experience what it feels like in your body.

- The breath is a constantly moving process. Each breath has its own life-cycle, starting with air coming into the nose or mouth, then moving down through the body all the way to the belly. Then a pause. Then the breath moves out again. Then a pause. Then the next in-breath. This whole cycle gives your attention something 'interesting' to explore – with each breath being different from the last one.

Developing awareness through the 'movement meditation'

As you may already have discovered, you don't have to be completely still to practise mindfulness. You can become fully aware of what's going on while in the midst of activity and movement. In fact, many people starting out in mindfulness find that it's easier this way. So it's worth introducing another core practice at this early stage: the 'movement meditation'. You will be invited to practise this, alternating it each day for a week or so with the 'waking up to yourself' meditation, before you move on to the next chapter.

This movement meditation does two main things:
1. Strengthens your ability to pay attention (concentration) and to bring back your attention (mindfulness) – just as in the 'waking up to yourself' meditation. The movements 'wake up' different parts of your body, and this helps to generate lots of sensations for you to focus your attention on. That's why some people find this easier than stationary meditation.

2. Realigns many of the body's muscles and joints, which helps to release stress in the body.

To practise this meditation, all you need to do is follow the audio guided meditation and refer to the detailed instructions below. However, here are a few helpful pointers about how to approach this meditation:

- The movements in this meditation are not for keeping fit or developing muscle tone. Rather they are another way to develop mindfulness and to release stress in the body. This being so, it's really important that you are gentle with yourself – it's not about going beyond some pain barrier. You know your body and its limits better than anyone else, so trust your body's wisdom about how far to go with any stretch or how long to hold it. If you have a problem with any part of your body – do check it out with a physician, and you may need to adapt a movement for yourself to avoid making the problem worse.

- Focus on the physical sensations. Try not to think *about* them – instead just notice how they feel.

- Also start to notice how your mind relates to the sensations. For example, if you notice a pain or tension, what kinds of thoughts or emotions come up for you?

- See if you can find an 'edge' for each movement – that is, the point at which you start to feel the first signs of tension or difficulty. Experiment with pushing that edge a bit further, without causing yourself pain. What happens in your mind when you do this?

Movement meditation instructions

Below is a description of each of the movements. It's best to practise this for the first few times while listening to the audio guide – details are at the end of the chapter.

1. Swing from side to side
Feet parallel and shoulder-width apart, knees bent, turning at the waist from side to side, allowing your arms to swing and your head to turn as you swing. Feeling the weight moving from one foot to the other.

2. Rotate the hips
Feet parallel and shoulder-width apart, hands on hips. Rotating the hips first one way, then the other.

3. Rotating the shoulders
Feet together. Lifting up the shoulders towards the ears and then back down. Letting arms dangle to the sides. First forwards rotations, then backwards.

4. Reaching up to the sky
Feet a few inches apart. Reaching up towards the sky first with one hand, then the other. Feeling the stretch down each side of the body. Keeping the centre of the body as still as you can. Pausing the movement – bringing the upper arms out to the sides, forearms pointing up. Resuming the stretches, and then gently allowing your arms to come back to your sides.

5. Holding a sphere
Feet shoulder-width apart, knees slightly bent, allowing the arms to float up in front of you as though you are holding a big sphere. Turning at the waist from side to side, allowing the arms to move with the body, and feeling the weight moving from one leg to the other. Gradually making the movements smaller until you come to rest, still with the arms up, and facing forward. Holding this position for a moment, then

letting the arms gently float down.

6. *Standing still*
Feet together, knees slightly bent. Closing your eyes. Noticing the contact with the ground. Noticing your breathing.

Starting to get to know yourself

Hopefully you are already getting a clear idea of the aims and benefits of mindfulness training: it's about engaging the 'being' mode of your mind to deal more effectively with certain problems or emotions that your autopilot isn't best equipped for. It's about seeing things more clearly.

One of the things you will start to see more clearly is *yourself*. This is where mindfulness training gets really interesting (not that it's been boring so far, hopefully!).

As you do the two core practices described above, you will notice how often your mind might wander off. It's as if the mind has a mind of its own. It jumps from one thing to the next – and gets scattered all over the place. This is most likely to happen when the mind is either pushing something unpleasant away (e.g. a pain in the body, a sad memory, or a worry about the future), or holding on to something pleasant (e.g. thinking about the chocolate bar you are going to have after the meditation!). See if you can notice this tendency as you continue working with these practices. And if you do notice it, don't give yourself a hard time – it is just how the human mind has evolved, so there is nothing wrong with you.

What's even more interesting is starting to *notice the kinds of places your mind habitually tends to wander off to* – and the kinds of thoughts, emotions and body sensations that accompany this. For example, you might notice that you tend to have a lot of thoughts about things on your to do list (i.e. thinking about the future). That might be accompanied by an emotion of anxiety, and you might be able to locate this feeling in your body – maybe a knot in your stomach, or tightness in your chest.

Noticing where your mind tends to wander off to

Noticing all this means you are really getting to know yourself and how your mind habitually operates. This kind of self-knowledge is the solid foundation on which you can make real changes in your life. While you might want to be able to change things right now, you are encouraged for now just to stay with the experience of what you are discovering about yourself. The good news is that this very act of staying with the experience is precisely what will enable things to change positively. That's going to be the focus of the next two chapters.

Short summary of this chapter

Mindfulness is about two things – first, training the mind to pay attention ... *and* to pay attention to your attention. And secondly, it's about a different way of being – seeing things as they really are, and opening up the broadest perspectives.

The primary mindfulness tool is meditation. This develops your ability to concentrate and focus on one thing at a time. Its ultimate aim is to develop your overall awareness – and it uses concentration as the main tool.

In the 'waking up to yourself' meditation, you are training two skills:

1. *Concentration or 'absorption'.* This is your ability to pay attention to your experience. You just notice what you notice. Don't force your concentration, rather allow your mind to become naturally *absorbed* in the sensations.

2. *Mindfulness.* This is *the ability to notice what is happening to your attention.* Your mind will wander, that's natural. Each time it happens, you just bring your attention back to your body/breath with kindness and patience.

The main aim of this practice is to become aware, and not to make relaxation happen. But if you are very agitated, stressed or restless, you can do some conscious deeper belly breathing to help you establish some calm. Some people also find that counting their breath helps them stay focused. So, you breathe in, and breathe out, and say silently to yourself 'One', then breathe in and out again and count two, and so on all the way up to ten, and then go back to one.

You don't have to be completely still to practise mindfulness. The movement meditation does two main things:

1. Strengthens your ability to pay attention (concentration) and to bring back your attention (mindfulness)
2. Realigns many of the body's muscles and joints, which helps to release stress in the body.

Some helpful pointers about how to approach this meditation:

*   Focus on the physical sensations.
*   Notice how your mind relates to the sensations.
*   See if you can find an 'edge' for each movement.

Mindfulness is ultimately about seeing things more clearly – including yourself. As you start to practise more, you will see how your mind jumps about a lot from one thing to another, especially when it is either pushing something unpleasant away, or holding on to something pleasant. Start to notice this tendency. You can also start to notice the kinds of places your mind habitually tends to wander off to – and the kinds of thoughts, emotions and body sensations that accompany this. When you do this, you are really getting to know yourself – and that's the foundation for making changes in your life.

Home practice before the next chapter

To stream or download the audio guided meditations listed below, go to: risingminds.org.uk/mindfulness

1. **Alternate each day** between these two practices:
- 'Waking up to yourself' meditation – follow the instructions on the audio guided meditation.
- 'Movement meditation' – follow the audio instructions and refer to the descriptions in this chapter

2. **Keep doing a routine activity mindfully** – like brushing your teeth or making a cup of tea

3. **Do something different**: take a slightly different route to work or a regular appointment. Notice things around you.

4. **Events journal**: in your journal keep a simple diary for a few significant events that happen (pleasant or unpleasant ones). For each event, jot down a few words about three aspects – thoughts, emotions and body sensations. See the example on the next page.

Event	Thoughts	Emotions	Body sensations
What happened?	What automatic thoughts came up?	What emotions came up?	What body sensations did I notice?
Someone bumped into me on the street	*People are so rude*	*Anger*	*Tension in my neck and shoulders*
My boss paid me a compliment	*I'm good at my job*	*Satisfaction*	*Relaxation in my body, particularly in my belly*

Chapter 3
The B of the ABC: Being with your experience, part 1 – Working with your thoughts

The first two chapters looked at what mindfulness is, why it's so helpful in everyday life, and how to start practising it. The focus was on the A of the ABC of mindfulness – Awareness of your experience. This first stage has been about using simple meditation and mindful exercises to help you notice your direct, moment-by-moment experience – particularly through awareness of sensations in the body.

*The focus is now moving to the B of mindfulness: Being with your experience. In a sense, this is simply a deepening of the first step of Awareness. In order to become more deeply aware of your experience, you need to be able to find a way to **stay with** it, including when it's unpleasant. As set out in the last chapter, this isn't always easy because the human mind doesn't like unpleasant experience and tries to push it away. This automatic response is understandable, but not always helpful, because it means you don't get the chance to fully understand what's happening, or the range of options available to you in any given situation.*

Really being with your experience when it's unpleasant can seem quite challenging at first. And so it requires a lot of patience, and kindness towards yourself. But be assured that, by following the steps and practices in this book, the effort is

worth it – as it can open up whole new perspectives for you.
Learning how to be with your experience can be broken down
into two stages:

1. ***Working with thoughts:*** *Noticing how your experiences*
   are created by the interlinking patterns of your
   thoughts and moods. You do this by watching your
   thoughts more carefully, and seeing the effect they
   have on your emotions. That's going to be the focus of
   this chapter.

2. ***Acceptance:*** *Cultivating an attitude of kindly*
   acceptance towards all experience, especially difficult
   experiences, instead of pushing them away. That will
   be the focus of Chapter 4.

Thoughts can become the master of you

Your mind is always trying to make sense of things

The starting point for this chapter is an understanding of how
your mind always wants to make sense of things. It receives
'information' through your senses – all that you see, hear,
touch, taste and smell. And then it automatically works in the
background to build up an accurate picture of what is going
on, based on this information.

This happens every time something happens to you, and
along the way your mind then draws up a whole data-bank of
'patterns' and 'rules' about how things work. These patterns
and rules are the basis for thoughts.

Let's illustrate this through a simple and fascinating exercise.
Read the following sentences one at a time. Try not to read
them all at once: pause briefly after each and see what your

understanding is of what's being described:

1. Sue likes eating vegetables.
(Pause)

2. Sue particularly likes courgettes.
(Pause)

3. Sue hates the taste of courgettes – she just likes the look of them.
(Pause)

4. Sue is a cat.

Most people when they read this find that their assumption about what is being described changes substantially as they go along. After the first two sentences you are likely to assume Sue is a person, and that she likes eating courgettes. Then it turns out she just likes the *look* of courgettes. And then, finally, it's revealed that Sue is a cat!

This example shows how the mind wants to fit things into pre-established patterns. For instance, in the example above, most people would have a pattern for thinking that Sue is a person's name, and not a cat's! So then you may get a bit of a jolt when it's shown that this pattern is being broken.

This powerful inbuilt urge to make sense of things is a legacy of the 'autopilot' mode that evolved in humans' prehistoric past, as described in the first two chapters. The human mind developed to solve problems in order to protect against danger. And to do that these patterns and rules needed to be formed, to allow for predictions of what might happen in future situations. For example, the experience of a wild animal chasing you would lead you to form this rule: wild animals = dangerous and to be avoided! This whole mental process happens unconsciously in the background.

You experience the world not as it is, but as you are

Your mind tries to fit each and every experience that you have into these pre-established patterns or rules. So strong is this tendency that if something happens that doesn't seem to fit, you are often more likely to get completely thrown by it, rather than altering the original pattern. As a result, you often end up not seeing things as they actually are, but rather through the lens of what you have yourself become, due to the unconscious conclusions you have drawn.

For example, let's imagine someone who doesn't have a very good opinion of themselves. If a friend or colleague pays them a compliment, rather than taking it at face value, they may instead think, 'they're only saying it because they want to get me to do something for them.' It can be seen here that the fundamental 'rules' at play in the person's mind are: 'I am not a very good person,' and 'People don't think much of me.' These are so fixed that the person isn't able to consider the possibility that the compliment was genuinely meant. Rather than changing the fundamental rules in their mind – perhaps to something like 'I have some good qualities,' or 'Some people think well of me,' instead they choose to read an ulterior motive into the compliment.

Mental patterns lead to emotions

So these patterns and rules become very deeply ingrained in your mind, and become the basis for a lot of your behaviour, thinking and decision-making. Your mind automatically refers to them in every experience and situation you are in: and in applying them it attempts to make meaning out of the event.

And here's the really important point: the meaning your mind makes will have an effect on how you feel. There's a simple formula that explains this phenomenon:

Situation + Interpretation → Emotion

Let's take an example to illustrate this point. Read the following scenario a couple of times. When you get to the end, notice any emotions that you feel.

You are walking down the street. You see a friend walking on the other side of the street. You wave at your friend. Your friend doesn't wave back or acknowledge you, and just carries on walking.

How does this scenario make you feel? Perhaps you feel sad, or angry, or hurt. Or even amused. Or perhaps other feelings. Or maybe nothing much at all. What you feel in fact depends on your own particular mental 'patterns' or 'rules' – in other words, the interpretation or automatic thoughts that you have about the situation. On the next page are some examples of possible interpretations and the likely emotions that may result from them.

Interpretation (or automatic thoughts)	Emotion that may result
The person I thought was my friend isn't really my friend after all, because they just ignored me.	Sadness, hurt
My friend is so absorbed in themselves that they didn't even notice me.	Anger
My friend is having a difficult time and so they didn't notice me.	Concern
My friend often has their head in the clouds!	Amusement
Stuff happens!	No particular emotion

Situation + Interpretation → Emotion

You can probably think of many other interpretations and resulting emotions. But the key point here is that the very same situation can give rise to a whole range of different emotions due to the particular interpretation you come up with. You may also come up with very different interpretations depending on your mood at the time. As seen in the first chapter, this is because of the very strong link between thoughts and feelings (or moods).

Remember, this whole process is happening unconsciously: your autopilot automatically digs out one or more patterns and rules from your data-bank and applies it to the situation, and that gives rise to an emotion.

Habitual thoughts and habitual emotions

In itself, this is no problem – you need your 'autopilot' mode to help you get through life. But often the patterns or rules that the mind automatically selects most frequently will lead to unpleasant emotions. Before you know it, you may feel fed up, or anxious, or low. You can't see how you got there. And you may end up there so frequently that it just becomes habitual to feel this way. The 'double whammy' part of this is that when the difficult emotion becomes habitual, it then reinforces the original pattern or rule that brought about the emotion in the first place. So then the mind digs it up even more often, leading to you feeling even more difficult emotions, and so the vicious cycle goes on.

The irony here is that you formed these patterns/rules in an attempt to make sense of the world, and to stay safe within it. And yet they can end up becoming the cause of so much suffering.

The role that memory plays

It's worth mentioning here the vital role that memory plays in this whole process of *Situation + Interpretation → Emotion*. In fact, if you had no memory, the process couldn't happen at all. It's memory that allows you to build up over time the databank of patterns and rules that give rise to automatic interpretations and thoughts. So whenever something happens, you refer back to the past to see if the present is shaping up in the same way.

What's most interesting, though, is the way your mood can affect the way you retrieve memories. Normally, when you are feeling OK, you are able to retrieve quite specific memories about certain events – including the day, time and place. However, if you are feeling low, tired or anxious, you are often only able to remember a general sense of what happened. Research shows that the more people have this kind of over-general memory, the harder they find it to let go of difficult things from the past, and the more they are affected by difficult things happening in the present. It's as if the past gets frozen and stuck in the mind. This is often what is going on when people go through periods of depression or anxiety.

Here's an example of this. Imagine someone who has just failed an exam. Understandably, they feel disappointed. But that disappointment doesn't shift, even after a few months. They continue to feel very low about it. They feel like a failure, like this is the 'story' of their life – it's just one big failure. In reality, there have been a few limited specific incidents from their past where they did fail a test of some kind. But in their current low mood, they are not able to remember the specific details of these isolated incidents. Instead they just have a general memory of 'failing'. Not only that, they are also blocking out a whole host of other situations where they passed a test or a challenge with flying colours. If they could remember all the specific details of all of these events —good and bad — they would be better able to see this most recent exam failure in a wider context, and so not feel so downhearted about it for so long.

You each have your own 'brand' of unhelpful patterns and thoughts

Human beings share many common experiences, and so tend to have very similar kinds of patterns and rules in the mind.

For example, here are some common thoughts that people have when they feel stressed: 'Something has got to change, or else …'; 'there is something wrong with me'; 'there's something wrong with everyone else'; 'this is my fault'; 'this is someone else's fault.' Or when people feel very happy, common thoughts might be: 'Life is pretty good'; 'I am a pretty good person'; 'I like other people.'

However, while humans have a common heritage, everyone is also a unique individual. As a result, each of you will have your particular 'brand' of habitual patterns and thoughts. It can be very interesting and revealing to start to see what some of your own particular habits of mind are.

Loosening the grip of thoughts

Perhaps what you have read so far in this chapter is making you feel a bit downhearted? It's as if your mind is working against you sometimes — keeping you trapped in a loop of unhelpful patterns of thoughts and feelings.

But don't despair. As you may have already read between the

lines, you don't actually have to believe everything your mind tells you. The interpretation you are making of a situation is based on all those patterns and rules your mind has formed, because the mind loves to keep everything organised and codified. But those patterns and rules – and all the thoughts that come with them – are very often not at all accurate.

In other words: **your thoughts are *not facts***. *This is an absolutely essential point at this stage in your mindfulness training.*

You have become so accustomed to your thoughts and interpretations over many years of them being there that they can often feel like the absolute truth. But the actual truth is that *thoughts are merely events happening in your mind,* just like an itch is an event in your body. And just as an itch passes in time, so too will your thoughts pass in time. We'll come back to this in a moment.

This doesn't mean that everything you think is wrong, or has no truth in it at all. Rather, this is a cue to help you start to relate to your thoughts in different ways. And this is where your mindfulness training gets down to the real nitty-gritty of changing long-established unhelpful habits and patterns. Ultimately it's about changing how you relate to *everything* that ever happens to you.

Using mindfulness to disentangle from unhelpful thoughts

It's tempting to think that the way to get rid of unhelpful thoughts is to confront them with other more sensible thoughts and cool logic. Sometimes this might kind of work, for a while. But more often than not, it doesn't actually get rid of the unhelpful thought for good – rather it just puts it off for a while – only for it to come back again, sometimes even more strongly. Or you just end up getting into an endless silent argument with yourself, leaving you feeling confused and exhausted.

Mindfulness teaches you to deal with thoughts in a very different way that's far more effective. This way is not about trying to *get rid* of those thoughts. Rather it's about *stepping outside* them, and simply watching them come and go, and unfold in their own natural way. For many people brought up in the modern West, where 'thinking' is often given supremacy over other ways of solving problems, this alternative approach can seem counterintuitive. But research is showing increasingly that it is the most effective antidote to negative thinking. As such, it's also the kindest way to work with difficult thoughts.

The 'working with your thoughts' meditation

So how do you actually step outside thoughts and watch them come and go? The best way to practise this is in meditation – using the 'working with your thoughts' meditation, which you will be invited to practise several times before you move on to the next chapter. The audio guided meditation (details at the end of the chapter) will take you through the various stages, but here's an overview of what happens:

Stage 1: Awareness of your body and breath (as in the 'waking up to yourself' meditation). You notice what you notice in your actual experience. You notice how sensations come and go, and change.

Stage 2: Noticing sounds. The reason for using sounds in this stage is that they are actually a lot like thoughts. If you allow yourself to listen to sounds and resist the temptation to label or identify them, you will notice how sounds come and go, and change and vary as time goes by. They are simply passing events. Thoughts are exactly the same in their nature. So this stage of the meditation helps you prepare for the next one ...

Stage 3: Noticing thoughts. In this stage, you simply notice thoughts coming and going, like clouds passing across the sky. This stage is vital in starting to become aware of your thoughts – to bring them into your conscious awareness, rather than them lurking in the shadows and controlling you without you knowing. So by noticing the thoughts, you start to get more distance from them. You can start to see that they are simply part of the patterns that your mind has built up over many years. As this happens, you are not completely in their grip. You get to notice more and more the most frequent kind of thoughts you tend to have, which may be different at different times. You can also see how one thought tends to lead to another, and then another – in a whole chain that unravels in a split second. And finally, you can start to notice how all your different thoughts tend to leave you feeling, both in your body and in your emotions.

Watching thoughts coming and going

Working with your thoughts outside meditation

As you've seen already, meditation isn't the only way to practise mindfulness. Meditation is where you can do the most intensive work to change old habits of mind. But that work can continue out of meditation, throughout your daily life. And this can include working with your thoughts.

There is a range of simple techniques you can use as you start to notice more of the most frequent kind of thoughts that you have, particularly the unhelpful ones that lead to difficult emotions. What all these techniques have in common is that they challenge the part of your mind that wants to believe that your thoughts are absolutely true. They take various approaches to put more distance between you and the thought.

As you practise and learn mindfulness – especially through the meditations – you will naturally start to become more aware of the kinds of thoughts that you have most often. You will get more 'tuned in' to your thinking, and will start to notice how certain difficult thoughts keep cropping up, again and again.

As this happens, you can deliberately choose one of the following techniques to work with a thought when it pops up. You can do this all in your imagination. Or it can be helpful to write things down. See what works best for you.

- *Using your wise mind*: Ask yourself where this thought takes you if you just go along with it, and what its impact on your behaviour is.

- *Remind yourself of the nature of your mind*: Pause and reflect on the fact that your mind is like a very good story teller that can make you believe anything. But it's still only a story.

- *Metaphor*: Imagine that the thoughts you are having are like clouds passing across a sky, or leaves floating down a stream.

- *Making light of the thought*: In your head (or even out loud!) put on a silly voice (e.g. a cartoon voice) to repeat the thought over and over again till it sounds ridiculous.

- *Giving the thought form:* In your mind's eye, sense the thought's form and location, its sound, and speed.

- *Noticing*: Rather than just having the thought, instead *notice* that you are having the thought. Say to yourself: 'I notice that I am having the thought that ...'

Working with emotions in the same way

It's been shown already how thoughts and emotions are very closely linked. In fact, in some psychological approaches they are seen as almost one and the same thing. To be precise, a thought first pops up in the unconscious mind (i.e. you don't know you are starting to have the thought). Before the thought makes its way into the conscious mind (i.e. you become aware of the thought), the emotional 'tone' of it leaks into your awareness. So, often the first sign of a thought is an emotional feeling. This means that you can work with your emotions in a very similar way to how you work with your thoughts. So, just as a thought is simply a passing event, and not a fact, so too emotions can be allowed simply to come and go. In other words, *you are not your emotions*. This enables you to make a vital shift from the statement 'I am angry' to 'I feel angry,' or even one step further to 'I notice that I feel angry.' These differences may seem very subtle, but they illustrate the distance you can put between yourself and your thoughts and emotions when you practise mindfulness. The next chapter will look in more depth at how to work with difficult emotions and feelings.

Working with your thoughts is truly being with your experience

Working with your thoughts and emotions in the way described above is the start of the B of the ABC of mindfulness: Being with your experience. That's because by getting intimately familiar with your thoughts, noticing them with kindness, and learning to disentangle yourself from the more unhelpful ones, you are getting to the heart of your actual experience rather than automatically trying to get away from it. The next chapter will look at the other main way to be with your experience – acceptance.

'Mini meditation': three-step breathing space

So far on this mindfulness programme, you've practised two main meditations – the 'waking up to yourself' meditation, and the movement meditation. Hopefully you're already noticing the benefits from practising these regularly.

Sometimes, however, you may feel the need to get those benefits when you don't have time to do a longer meditation. The great thing about mindfulness practice is that you can use simple awareness of your body and your breath *at any time* to help you come back into the present moment. All you need to do is pause for a moment – and notice your body and your breath.

If you've got a few minutes, you can also use the three stages of the three-step breathing space. This is like a mini-meditation you can do whenever you feel like it. It's best done sitting down – but you can also do it standing up.

1. *Awareness*: Adopting a posture that is both relaxed and alert. Taking a few slightly deeper breaths, and as you breathe in imagining the breath moving up and giving your back and neck an uplift. As you breathe

out, imagining it travelling down your front. Now tuning in to yourself. Getting an overall sense of your experience right now. Asking yourself: What am I thinking? What mood am I in? What can I feel in my body?

2. *Gathering*: Bringing the focus of your awareness onto your breathing. Following your breathing, as best you can, with kindness and patience.

3. *Expanding*: Broadening out your awareness to include your whole body and facial expression. Noticing anything else coming to you through your senses: what you can hear, see, smell, taste and touch?

Mindful planning using the three-step breathing space

When you train in mindfulness, you are training your mind to pay attention to your experience in the here and now. But this doesn't mean that mindfulness is only about being aware of the present, in some kind of vacuum. You can turn the same skills of paying attention – in a clear, calm and focused way – towards the future, whether that's today, this week, this month, or this year.

At the beginning of each day you can spend a few quiet moments consciously planning the day ahead. You can also set aside brief moments for relaxed reflection throughout your day – giving your mind a chance to process what's already happened, and checking in with yourself as to how you feel. Based on that, you can amend your day's plan (where possible) – responding flexibly to your experience and energy levels. The three-step breathing space is a great way to prepare yourself for this kind of relaxed, open reflection and planning.

An even shorter meditation – the mindful minute

There may be times when you feel the need to calm down, or be re-energised, and you haven't even got a few minutes. And you may not be somewhere where it's appropriate to close your eyes. If so, then you can still use the principles of mindfulness in as little as a minute or even 30 seconds – with your eyes open:

1. Stop what you're doing.
2. Notice two things you can see.
3. Notice two things you can hear.
4. Notice two things your body is touching (e.g. your feet on the floor, your back against the chair, the touch of your clothes on your skin).
5. Allow all of these things to merge into a general awareness of what's going on right now in and around you.

Meditation tip: treat yourself with kindness

One of the most important things to mention about meditation is the *attitude* you take towards yourself when you practise it. Hopefully you have already got the message loud and clear (from this book and the audio guided meditations) that it's best if you can adopt an attitude of kindness and patience.

It's impossible to overstate the importance of developing this kindly attitude towards yourself during meditation. We'll be looking at this in more depth in the next chapter, but for now here are a few pointers to how you can develop such an attitude.

Don't set your expectations too high: by learning mindfulness you are starting to challenge and change very long-standing habits of mind. This will take time. So don't expect dramatic changes instantly. That will only lead to disappointment.

Little and often: it's much better to do a little bit of practice every day (even if that's only 10 or 15 minutes), rather than leave it for days and then try and cram in lots in one go. Regular practice will help you form new positive mental habits.

A wandering mind is a sign that you are a normal human being. It's very common for newcomers to meditation to get very frustrated with themselves when they notice that their mind constantly wanders off from the object of the meditation (body, breath, sounds or thoughts). It's as if they have 'failed' in the meditation. This couldn't be further from the truth. First, it's completely natural that your mind should wander off, because it has evolved to be a highly alert sensor of danger – constantly scanning and checking what's going on around it. Secondly, the very act of noticing that your mind has wandered off means that you are in fact learning to be mindful. Each time you notice the mind has wandered off, you are building and strengthening the neural pathways in the parts of your brain that are associated with paying relaxed attention. Research shows that this leads, in turn, to greater wellbeing and clearer thinking.

Short summary of this chapter

The 'autopilot' mode that evolved in humans' prehistoric past to help avert danger has left a legacy in the mind: a strong tendency to make sense of things and to build up an accurate picture of what's going on. How your mind interprets a situation then has an effect on how you feel:

Situation + Interpretation → Emotion

The same situation can give rise to a whole range of different emotions depending on what your mind makes of it. For many people the interpretation that the mind automatically selects most frequently leads to unpleasant emotions. If this happens repeatedly those emotions themselves become habitual, just like the thoughts that lead there in the first place. A habitual emotion then itself reinforces the original mental pattern, leading to more difficult emotions. And so the vicious cycle goes on. Memory plays a vital role in this whole process. It's as if the past gets frozen and stuck in the mind.

Human beings, with a common heritage, tend to have similar kinds of patterns and rules. But as unique individuals, everyone has their own particular 'brand' of habitual patterns and thoughts.

You have become so accustomed to your thoughts and interpretations over many years that they can often feel like the absolute truth. But the actual truth is that **thoughts are not facts**. *They are merely events happening in your mind*: they come and go. This doesn't mean that everything you think is wrong, or has no truth in it at all. Rather, it's a cue to help you start to relate to your thoughts in different ways.

Confronting unhelpful thoughts with cool logic often doesn't work – it doesn't get rid of them, but just puts them off for a while. The mindful way to loosen the grip of thoughts is to *step outside* of them, and simply watch them come and go in their own natural way. This is far more effective.

In the 'working with your thoughts' meditation, you start with grounding and settling down through awareness of your body and breath. Then you notice sounds – which, like thoughts, are simply passing events. This helps prepare you for the final stage of noticing thoughts coming and going, like clouds passing across the sky. You notice the most frequent kind of thoughts you tend to have, and how one thought tends to lead to another. You also notice how different thoughts lead to different emotions and sensations in the body.

Home practice before the next chapter

To stream or download the audio guided meditations listed below, go to: risingminds.org.uk/mindfulness

1. **Alternate each day** between these two practices:

    *   **'Working with your thoughts' meditation** – follow the instructions on the audio meditation.

    *   **'Movement meditation'** – follow the instructions on the audio meditation. Notice particularly the thoughts that come up when you do the movements.

2. **Working with your thoughts away from meditation** – try using some of the techniques detailed in this chapter to help you work with unhelpful thoughts that you notice.

3. **Mini meditations**: three-step breathing space and/or the mindful minute – practise this whenever you have a spare few moments: either on your own, or listening to the audio.

4. **Do something different**: instead of watching your favourite TV show, choose something different to do -

(don't worry, you can record it and watch it another time!).

Journaling: In your journal jot down some notes about how you are relating to your thoughts. If you feel stuck as to what to write, these questions might help:

- *Am I taking my thoughts to be facts?*
- *How do my thoughts affect my behaviour?*
- *Are there common threads through many of my thoughts?*

Chapter 4
The B of the ABC: Being with your experience, part 2 – Acceptance

In the first half of this mindfulness training programme you have been training your muscles of attention – becoming aware of your moment-by-moment experience in your body and mind. That's the A of the ABC of mindfulness: Awareness.

Then in the last chapter, the focus moved into the B of the ABC: Being with your experience. The first stage of this is to watch and investigate thoughts carefully. Thoughts are the result of your mind's automatic desire to make sense of everything around you. Some resulting thoughts may not be very helpful or even 'true'. The best way out of this problem is to observe your thoughts (and the emotions that are linked to them), seeing them as mere events in your mind that come and go. This is far more effective than trying to remove or suppress those thoughts. By working with thoughts in this way, you are naturally starting to learn how to really 'be' with your experience, which is the essence of mindfulness practice.

In this chapter, you are going to move further into this process of 'being with your experience'. This is about exploring what all experience actually feels like, at a deep physical and emotional level in the body. The focus will be on how human beings tend to 'push away' difficult experience, and 'hold on to' pleasant experience – and why this isn't really in your best interests. To counteract this tendency, you'll see how you can learn to accept more of your experience, and turn towards it with patience, curiosity and kindness. With this, you are now moving into the beating heart of mindfulness practice.

Discovering what's really there

In your mindfulness training so far, by paying attention to your experience in a new way, hopefully you have started to see the rumours and half-truths that your mind often runs on. By simply noticing this, you are learning how to put some distance between 'you' and these habitual thoughts and the emotions associated with them. This enables you to delve beneath that whole layer of stories and ideas – and to get to what is actually there in your body as raw physical sensations.

As you may already have been noticing, every experience you have falls somewhere on a spectrum of pleasure/pain. Some experiences are very pleasurable, some are very unpleasant, and the rest are somewhere in between. It is all there to be felt – including unpleasant experiences – and all for good reason. There will be more on this shortly.

Trying to fix or remove unpleasant experience doesn't work

As explained already, when your autopilot mode notices unpleasant physical sensations/emotions or a 'problem', it automatically tries to fix, ignore or remove them. It's entirely natural and understandable that this happens: the mind has evolved this way to keep you safe. Human beings go through life learning all sorts of ways to do this. Some of them can kind of work for a while. They might include common 'habits' like use of alcohol, drugs, food, work, exercise, sex, etc. In their different ways, they each dull the pain, or provide a distraction, for a while at least. And in themselves there's nothing wrong with a lot of them – in moderation. But eventually, if overused, they simply stop working and can even make matters worse due to the dependency that's formed. And trying to fix or remove the original problem – and then finding that this doesn't work – can often lead to exhaustion or a deep-down conviction that nothing can be done about it, or that there's something fundamentally wrong.

It's better to turn towards and accept unpleasant experience

Instead of carrying on in this way – and bashing your head against a brick wall – you can choose to relate differently to the difficult sensation/emotion/thought. And this way is all about *acceptance* – of yourself and the problem. This involves first just noticing that strong automatic desire to drive away or suppress the difficulty. Then it's about letting it go, as best you can, and instead turning towards the difficulty – and exploring it with patience, kindness and curiosity. Of course, this can seem very challenging at times. So the key here is about taking small steps.

Acceptance is an act of courage and kindness, not resignation or denial

The word 'acceptance' might evoke a sense of resigning yourself to something, giving up, or suppressing your feelings. This is *not* what is meant by acceptance. Rather, it's about noticing how a situation or experience actually is, and then consciously choosing to experience it fully. It's about allowing things to be as they are.

This is the very opposite of suppressing your emotions. It's about feeling them deeply, particularly in your body. It's entirely natural for human beings to have a very wide range of emotions: they all have their place and want to be felt. For example, if you have lost something important to you, it's natural that you would feel sadness. Sadness is not a bad thing to experience in itself, it's only your mind that might tell you so. The same goes for other 'difficult' emotions, like anger, hurt, or frustration.

By allowing yourself to feel these emotions, in your body, you are able to experience the fullness of your human nature and you strengthen your capacity to deal with the problems that life throws up. This is exactly what is meant by 'resilience' – the ability to withstand difficulties and to recover from setbacks. And the best training for it is to accept what is actually going on in your experience, rather than what you might like to happen.

This process of fully turning towards your feelings requires both *strength* and *kindness* towards yourself. The meditation for this chapter invites these two vital qualities of mind to flourish.

Original and added layers of emotion

It's worth making a simple point here about layers of emotion. You can't choose to stop experiencing original layers of difficult emotions – such as fear, anger, or sadness – which naturally arise in response to circumstances. These original emotions are part of the human condition. However, you do have a choice about how you respond to them. And the way that you respond will affect what the next layer of emotion is. As you'll see in the rest of this chapter, an attitude of acceptance towards that original difficult layer will give you a better chance of ensuring that the next layer of emotion is not so difficult or unpleasant.

Turning towards the difficult and learning from it

Treating your emotions as trusted guides for action

Another way of describing the process of acceptance is that you are making friends with these difficult 'original' emotions, rather than treating some of them as dreaded enemies. You are giving them the chance to communicate something useful to you, just as you might let a trusted friend give you advice.

For example, you might notice that you are feeling angry, and by allowing yourself to feel that fully, you realise that it's due to something someone has said to you, and that you need to address some difficulty with them. This doesn't mean that you have to give full vent to that anger, by shouting or raging at them. This would be *acting out* the emotion through an automatic reaction, which is likely to make the situation worse. This is very different from allowing yourself to *feel* the emotion fully, and giving it some space. It's like pressing the pause button before deciding what to do. By doing this, the subsequent action that you take is far more likely to improve the situation. This is about allowing a wise response to emerge – one that is genuinely suited to the situation. There will be more on this in the next chapter, with the C of the ABC of mindfulness – Choosing wise responses to your experience.

Nipping things in the bud

Learning to accept your experience enhances your ability to nip difficulties in the bud, before they grow into major problems. The key here is about noticing that very tendency to make things worse than they need be. So as your training in mindfulness deepens, you will increasingly notice how there is often first an original experience of difficulty. Then, the mind's automatic reaction – as already seen – is to try and fix it immediately, push it away, ignore it. But if you are able to simply *stay with* the original difficulty, then that automatic desire to push it away can diminish. You can never stop the difficult thought or emotion from arising in the first place (unless you are superhuman), but you do have the power to let it go after it has arisen.

It's worth illustrating this with the example of a chronic pain condition that comes and goes. Imagine that one morning, after a longish period of no pain, you notice a sharp pain. In an unmindful state, there are several ways you might automatically go with this. One would be to take a painkiller immediately in an attempt to block out the pain. Another would be to pretend not to have noticed the pain and unconsciously hope it doesn't come back. The problem with both of these approaches is that they are only postponing difficulty: the effects of the painkiller will wear off after a few hours; it won't be possible to pretend for very long there isn't pain.

A different – and more helpful – response would be straight away to acknowledge fully what is actually happening without instantly trying to fix it or ignore it. You can choose to notice the pain and pause a moment to allow it to be felt more fully. It may feel counterintuitive to feel the pain more fully, but it's the best-long term plan. You can breathe into it and allow the mind to explore it with kindness and curiosity – seeing if the experience of the pain changes as you give it more space.

Taking this approach will not necessarily remove the pain – as there may indeed be a physiological problem that needs treatment. But it can dramatically affect the relationship you have with the pain. By accepting the pain's existence, there is a better chance that it might not be so difficult to endure. It also means you're more likely to know how to adapt to the pain being there – perhaps altering the position you sit or stand in, or doing a particular exercise. You might also decide to take a painkiller – but as a conscious choice, rather than as a knee-jerk reaction.

By turning towards the physical experience in this way, you're also better placed to catch any automatic thoughts that come up. In this example, these could include: 'I thought this problem had gone away, but it's returned and it's worse than ever,' or 'This problem is ruining my life.' By noticing that you are having these thoughts, rather than them happening unseen in the background, you can prevent yourself going into a downward spiral where those negative thoughts make the original pain feel even worse, leading to worse negative thoughts, and so on.

Acceptance happens in the body

Throughout this programme, and this chapter, there has been a particular emphasis on awareness of body sensations. As you will see in the meditation, practising acceptance is about working with the body's response to difficulty, rather than trying to 'figure out' the difficulty in your thinking mind alone. The problem with the latter approach is that it can reinforce the mind's goal-oriented 'doing' mode, which is often the cause of the problem in the first place. Working with the body instead allows space between you and the problem – you are still working through the same raw material, but held within a different 'being' mode of mind. By working directly with the physical sensations, you will see how much they alter and change moment by moment – which is actually exactly the same with states of mind. It's also easier to identify when difficult emotions have been 'triggered' in you – as you become more familiar with the signs in your body (e.g. shallow breathing, rapid heartbeat, sickness in the stomach, etc.). And further, you get to see how the patterns of thinking explored in Chapter 3 are 'mirrored' by patterns in the body – which can show up as tension, stress or pain.

Acceptance applies to pleasant experiences as well

This chapter has been focusing on how to work more effectively with unpleasant experiences, by turning towards and accepting them. You might be surprised to hear that the same approach is very useful with pleasant experiences. So when you notice a pleasant sensation in your body, or have a thought that leaves you feeling positive and happy, allow yourself to feel that very fully – give it some space. There are two good reasons for doing this.

First, it allows you to appreciate simple and natural pleasures that arise without the need for too much external stimuli. You might get to learn in the process which simple activities give you pleasure – and this is really useful information for you about how to live your life. There will be more on this idea in the next chapter.

Secondly, you might notice how your mind wants to cling on to a pleasant experience for as long as possible. That's totally understandable: humans like pleasure! And this 'holding on' to pleasant experience may seem to be the opposite of 'pushing away' difficult experience. But it is actually the same phenomenon of *wanting things to be other than they are*. If you can learn to let the pleasant experience be there *for just as long as it naturally wants to*, rather than trying to nail it down for good, you are actually strengthening your ability to allow unpleasant experiences to fade away more easily.

For example, imagine you are enjoying a delicious meal. You can use your mindfulness skills of 'awareness' and 'being with' to fully savour the pleasure that the food is giving you. Explore and enjoy the tastes and textures in your mouth, or other pleasurable sensations in your body, wherever you notice them. Take a bit of extra time over this – it's easy to bolt food down very quickly without noticing it! You could even notice the food going all the way down into your stomach, and feel it nourishing you. Not only will this approach enhance the natural pleasure that the food gives you, it will also enable you to get a clearer sense when you are actually full – when eating any more won't really give you any more pleasure.

Knowing what to change and what not to change

As said before, acceptance doesn't mean resignation, giving up, or suppressing your feelings. Rather, it's about learning to notice how things actually are before deciding what to do. As you practise this more, you may start to get a clearer sense of which things you can influence and change, and which things are totally out of your control. Mindfulness teaches you how to make this distinction.

Here's an example of each – in both cases with something that you may notice is getting you down. So, if it's raining outside, there's nothing you can do about this – it's better to accept it, rather than let it get you down. But if you've had an argument with someone and said some things you regret, there might be something you can actively do to improve the situation and your mood. Perhaps you need to arrange to speak to them and clear the air.

Perhaps one of the biggest tricks to a good life is making the distinction between the things that you can change, and the things that you can't change and need to accept.

Knowing what to change and what not to change

How to practise acceptance in meditation

The 'acceptance' audio guided meditation will take you through the stages to practise what's been set out in this chapter. As you will see, the meditation encourages you to connect with the two vital qualities of *courage* and *kindness*. Here is a brief overview of what happens in the meditation:

Stage 1: Awareness of your body and breath (as in the 'waking up to yourself' meditation).

Stage 2: Connecting with your strength and kindness. Taking your attention into the areas around your belly (for courage) and your heart (for kindness), and allowing these natural qualities to be felt, even if only dimly.

Stage 3: Turning towards sensations in the body. Noticing particularly if there are strong sensations – pleasant or unpleasant – and if there is an urge to push them away or hold on to them. Exploring the sensations, using your imagination and your breath to help you stay with them. Saying to yourself: '*It's OK – whatever it is, it's OK. Let me feel it.*'

Stage 4: Reconnecting with strength and kindness. Coming back to your belly and heart area, in the context of awareness of your whole body.

Using the three-step breathing space to practise acceptance

The last chapter introduced the three-step breathing space as a mini-meditation to use whenever you feel the need to come back to your current-moment experience. This is particularly useful when you find yourself 'triggered' or facing some strong difficult feelings. You can do this in as little as a minute, or for longer if you are able. You follow the same steps as before, but with an emphasis on turning towards those strong feelings:

1. *Awareness*: Adopting a posture that is both relaxed and alert. Taking a few slightly deeper breaths, and as you breathe in imagining the breath moving up and giving your back and neck an uplift. As you breathe out, imagining it travelling down your front. Now tuning in to yourself. Getting an overall sense of your experience right now. What am I thinking? What mood am I in? What can I feel in my body?

2. *Gathering*: Bringing the focus of your awareness onto your breathing.

3. *Expanding*: Broadening out your awareness to include your whole body and facial expression, especially noticing any sense of discomfort, tension or resistance. As best you can, allow the sensations to be there, as they are in this moment. Breathe into them, and let them soften and open on the outbreath.

How to practise acceptance outside meditation

The previous chapter suggested a range of exercises and techniques you could use to work with your thoughts outside formal meditation. In a similar way, there are some exercises you can use to practise acceptance, particularly when you find yourself experiencing strong difficult emotions. All of them are designed to help you 'open up' and turn towards your experience, rather than push it away. As with the thoughts exercises, you can carry them out in your imagination, or write some things down. Again, see what works best for you.

Use imagery: If you find yourself struggling to fight off a difficult experience then, in your mind's eye, picture what it's like desperately trying to get out of quicksand, or fighting a monster that grows bigger each time you land a blow on it. In both cases, it's the struggling that's making things worse. How might it be to give up a futile struggle?

Being a curious scientist: Explore the difficult feeling as if you are a scientist examining a new object – what's its size, weight, shape, colour, texture, etc.? Describe it as objectively as you can.

Give yourself the choice to feel: Ask yourself which of these two scenarios you would *really* prefer – a) never to feel this feeling again, but at the same time never to have *any feelings at all*, and so never able to care about anything again; b) you can carry on caring about things, but you will get this feeling from time to time.

Normalising: Remind yourself that having this feeling means you are a normal human being with a full range of experience.

Wading through the swamp: Imagine that these difficult feelings are like wading through a swamp ... but that what lies ahead is the mountain that you really want to climb.

Short summary of this chapter

Your autopilot tries to fix, ignore or get rid of unpleasant experiences. It's why people can turn to things like alcohol, food, sex or over-work to push away difficult feelings. These can kind of work for a while. But trying to fix things eventually stops working, and can leave you feeling exhausted or inadequate.

You can choose to relate differently to difficult sensations, emotions or thoughts. This is about *acceptance*. It doesn't mean resignation, giving up or suppressing your feelings. Rather it's about noticing how things actually are, then choosing to turn towards them and feel them deeply in your body. This strengthens your ability to withstand difficulties and to recover from setbacks (resilience). This process of fully turning towards your feelings requires both *courage* and *kindness* towards yourself.

With mindfulness, you will increasingly notice how there is often first an original experience of difficulty, and then the mind's automatic reaction is to try and push it away. But if you are able to simply *stay with* the original difficulty, then that automatic desire to push it away can diminish. The best way to practise this is by noticing how your body responds to difficulties, rather than trying to figure it out in your thinking mind, which can't always solve things. Working with body responses allows space between 'you' and the 'problem' – so that you can process the same raw material, but with 'being' rather than 'doing' mode. It also means you get more familiar with signs in your body that you've been 'triggered'.

The same acceptance approach is useful with pleasant experiences. If you allow yourself to feel a pleasant sensation fully, two things can happen. First, you learn about appreciating simple pleasures that are available to you without the need for too much external stimuli. Second, you might notice how the mind wants to 'hold on' to pleasant experiences for as long as possible – and how this is part of the same phenomenon of *wanting things to be other than they are*.

Home practice before the next chapter

To stream or download the audio guided meditations listed below, go to: risingminds.org.uk/mindfulness

1. **Alternate each day** between these two practices:
- **'Acceptance' meditation** – follow the instructions on the audio meditation.
- **'Movement meditation'** – follow the audio instructions. Notice particularly if you get any strong difficult feelings or sensations, and notice how you relate to them. Can you allow them to be there without trying to fix them?

2. Practising acceptance away from meditation – try using some of the techniques outlined above to practise acceptance.

3. Three-step breathing space – use this whenever you get triggered or are experiencing some difficulty: either on your own, or using the audio.

4. Do something different – the next time you watch the news or read a newspaper, notice when you have a strong opinion about something. Then try constructing an argument that's totally the opposite.

Journaling: In your journal jot down some notes about what you notice when you allow yourself to turn towards all your experiences more. If you feel stuck as to what to write, these questions might help:

- *How do I tend to try and fix or block out difficult experiences?*
- *What happens when I allow myself to feel them more – even if only for a moment longer?*
- *What else might I be blocking out of my life by doing this?*

Chapter 5
The C of the ABC: Choosing wise responses

The previous two chapters focused on the B of the ABC of mindfulness: Being with your experience. This was first about how to work with your thoughts more effectively – investigating them and observing them come and go. Next, the focus was on how to explore what lies beneath those thoughts, in your body, as raw physical sensations. Then it's about turning towards those sensations with an attitude of kindly acceptance, as a much more effective approach than immediately trying to fix them – which is what the autopilot mode of mind tends to do.

This chapter now moves to the C of the ABC of mindfulness: Choosing wise responses to your experience. This is about gathering all the skills and new mental habits you have been building, and bringing them to bear very directly on your life: both in your day-to-day choices and actions, and in the bigger decisions you take about the overall direction of your life. It's about using mindfulness as the platform from which you can view yourself and your life in the broadest perspective. It's about finding out what truly promotes your wellbeing and a sense of purpose and direction in life.

Responding wisely, not reacting automatically

The good news is that in order to move on to the C of the ABC of mindfulness – and to make wise choices in life – you haven't got to learn any major new skills, or make some great concerted effort to become a better person. By learning the two first core skills of Awareness and Being with experience, you already have all you need to make naturally wise choices in your life.

That's because the fundamental basis for wise choices is the ability to become aware of autopilot and to see how it can often lead down unhelpful patterns of thinking and feeling. Perhaps you have already seen this in your life. If so, you may have noticed that something different can happen when you create a gap between an initial event and your next move. It's as if you press the pause button and in that gap you just notice how autopilot wants to automatically dictate what happens next. If you can just stay there a moment longer than usual, observe that strong compulsion, allow it to be there and to be felt in the body, then you are creating space for other courses of action to be considered.

This is what is meant by *responding wisely rather than reacting automatically*. By creating that gap, you are inviting in more creative, spontaneous thinking that can open up fresh perspectives. This process might only need a split second, or it might need longer – sometimes minutes or hours, or even days or weeks, depending on the issue. It's about giving things the time and space they need to be resolved in the most helpful way.

All the mindfulness training you have been doing so far has been leading here – to the moments throughout your day and your life when you make decisions that affect the quality of your life. And what you are hopefully finding is that the skills you are learning mean you are better placed to make wise choices that enhance the wellbeing of you and the people around you.

In a sense, nothing more need be said about this. You have the core mindfulness skills to prepare yourself to make wise choices, as there is no one-size-fits-all set of rules for what constitutes a wise choice. The mindfulness approach is about you finding *for yourself* what is most appropriate in any situation, and trusting your own experience, intuition and wisdom.

However, it's worth getting a bit more specific about the different aspects of what it means to choose wise responses. As such, what follows is also a description of the very real benefits of mindfulness practice, applied in a range of situations. They are helpful mental attitudes that naturally arise when you start to weave mindfulness into your life. Perhaps you are already seeing these clearly in your life.

Connecting with your values and purpose

As stated throughout this book, mindfulness leads to greater self-awareness. Knowing yourself well means seeing and appreciating your strengths, as well as coming to terms with your weaknesses. But, perhaps more importantly, it means identifying the core values by which you want to live. Values are guiding principles in life – they describe what you want to stand for, your purpose or sense of meaning in life. Whereas goals describe the places or achievements you want to reach, values are about the way in which you go about your life. You are more likely to be able to make wise choices in life if they are in accordance with your values. And mindfulness is the best way to enable you to identify what your values are, as it creates that calm space in which your clarity of purpose can arise.

Freedom	Achievement	Appreciation
Choice	Accomplishment	Acknowledgement
Empowerment	Excellence	Recognition
Independence	Productivity	Respect
Authenticity	Trust	Beauty
Truthfulness	Integrity	Magnificence
Honesty	Decency	Splendour
	Fairness	
Peace	Flow	Change
Calm	Ease	Challenge
Contentment	Effortlessness	Growth
Simplicity	Relaxation	Learning
Collaboration	Understanding	Love
Cooperation	Patience	Compassion
Participation	Tolerance	Kindness
Support	Forgiveness	
Connection	Contribution	Creativity
Community	Generosity	Expression
Friendship	Helpfulness	Imagination
	Service	
Determination	Passion	Play
Strength	Enthusiasm	Fun
Focus	Romance	Joy
Dynamism	Vitality	Humour
Knowledge	Order	Openness
Clarity	Accuracy	Curiosity
Insight	Efficiency	Spontaneity
		Flexibility
Adventure	Meaning	Wellbeing
Discovery	Purpose	Health
	Spirituality	

List of core values

On the facing page is a list of core values, each with other related values. You can spend some time reflecting on these – perhaps after a bit of meditation – and choosing the top ten that feel most important to the way you live your life.

If you find it hard to identify your top values, you might find some of the following processes helpful:

- *Contribution*: Ask yourself what you've done in the last year that you're most proud of. And what about the next year – what could you do that would give you most satisfaction? And in the next week, or day?

- *Writing your obituary*: This does not need to be a morbid exercise! It's a way of getting to the heart of what matters to you. Imagine that you have lived the best possible life for you. Now write your obituary/eulogy. This could be as far away in the future as you wish. To help you do this, some questions you could address are: What will you have achieved? What qualities will people most wish to celebrate in you? How will you have affected them?

- *Character strengths*: Which do you already have? Which do you want to develop?

- *Role models*: Whom do you look up to? What personal strengths or qualities do you admire?

- *Wealth*: You inherit a fortune – what would you do with it? Who would benefit and share? How would you act?

- *Disapproval*: What do you disapprove of in others, and so what would you do differently in their shoes?

Here's an example of how values can help you make wise choices. Imagine someone who identifies their top three values as independence, adventure and determination. If they were given the opportunity to take on some kind of risky but potentially rewarding project – professional or personal – they might feel emboldened to do so, based on a clear understanding that this is in line with the person they feel themselves to be. Someone else with the three top values of contentment, order and wellbeing may judge that itwouldn't be in keeping with these values to take on the risk. Of course, often you just know – deep down – whether something feels like a good or bad move for you. But at other times, when you're not so clear, it can help to check back with your values to get some extra guidance.

It's worth mentioning that your core values can change as you change. So it can be useful to do a 'values sort' every now and then. It's a good way of finding out exactly how you are in fact changing.

Connecting with values and purpose

Clearer thinking and better planning

Chapter 3 looked at how to work more effectively with your thoughts, particularly the automatic, repetitive ones that sometimes aren't very helpful. The fundamental point here is that thoughts are not facts – and that as you investigate them more, you can challenge them and ask yourself if they fit with the reality of the situation. By working mindfully in this way, you are allowing the possibility of new, more creative thoughts to arise – ones more aligned with how things actually are, not how you want or fear them to be. In other words, mindfulness promotes a better quality of thinking processes. In turn, better thinking processes lead to better planning, organisational and decision-making skills. The reason that mindfulness trains this skill is that it teaches you how to hold in your mind at the same time both a narrow focus (e.g. noticing just your left big toe) and a broad awareness (e.g. noticing the whole of your body). It also teaches you how to switch between the two. This translates into being able to pay attention to the detail while also seeing the big picture in any situation – a vital skill for planning and decision-making.

Here are a couple of examples – both a small day-to-day decision, and a larger one affecting the direction of one's life.

First, a small day-to-day decision. Let's imagine that you have a massive to do list, stuffed with work tasks and/or domestic chores. They all seem to have imminent deadlines, and you're feeling pressurised. And then you get a phone call from a friend who's in need of some kind of urgent support, which requires you to drop what you're working on right now. What do you do?

In an unmindful state of mind, several things may happen that may not be helpful, leaving you feeling even worse. You might rush into doing what your friend asks of you, without thinking much about the consequences, and all the time worrying that you're not getting through your urgent to do list. Or you might instantly tell your friend that you can't help because you've got too much to do, but then feel so guilty about this that you can't really concentrate on anything. Or you might feel altogether overwhelmed and simply freeze – not knowing what to do.

Instead, if you apply everything you've learned so far about mindfulness, you can take some pressure off in difficult situations like this. You can take a brief pause – a few minutes, or just 30 seconds (or even shorter, while you're actually speaking to your friend), and simply reconnect with yourself in your body, noticing the thoughts and emotions running through you. It's about buying yourself a bit of time to centre and ground yourself so you can think more clearly.

With that extra bit of time and space, you will probably find that some other wise options and steps become clear to you. In this case, you might realise that you need to find out a bit more about exactly what support is going to be most helpful for your friend, and how you can fit that in without being overwhelmed. You might choose to explain that you have limited time right now, but that you're willing to help, and will also have more time in a day or two. You may also revisit your to do list, and do some prioritising, so that you can see what is urgent and what can be delayed. For tasks that involve other people, or that you're doing for them, you may choose to check out what leeway there is on the timing. Other ideas that are best for the situation may also come to you when you take this kind of 'breathing space' to think more clearly.

Crucially, through mindfulness practice, you can also be clear with yourself about what is actually possible for you while still maintaining your own wellbeing and composure. Once you are clear about this with yourself, it's usually much easier to communicate this to others so that they understand where you're coming from.

Now let's look at bigger decisions. Let's imagine that you're considering a major life change – that could be moving location, starting a new career, getting married or going into a new relationship. No doubt you can think of your own examples. You've been deliberating about this potential change for a while. You find that you keep going round in circles in your head about the pros and cons of making the change. You may have written down a list of these, but still not felt clear about what to do. You may also have spoken to friends and family about it, and each of them has given you a different bit of advice and opinion. You're left feeling confused, stuck and unable to make a decision.

The mindful way of dealing with this kind of major decision could involve one or more of several related approaches:

- **Stepping outside the incessant flurry of thoughts** – be they facts, opinions, or possibilities – that surround the decision. When faced with big decisions, it's all too easy for the mind to get completely 'stuck' on it – so that there are constant thoughts going round. It can almost seem like you're having a non-stop argument with yourself about it, as you try hard to come up with the solution. This can be exhausting, and doesn't promote clear thinking. For your higher brain functions to work well when you need them to, it's essential to give them plenty of rest. So when you notice you're caught up in heavy thinking, trying to solve the problem, all you need to do is simply notice that it's happening. Then you can consciously choose to take your attention elsewhere – first of all, to your body and breathing, and then you might choose to do some other engaging activity that has nothing to do with this decision.

- **Finding wisdom in your body** – at the heart of mindfulness is the ability to use the whole of your body/mind system to good effect in life. People in the modern West are generally brought up to solve problems with the brain alone. But when you practise the whole-body awareness that mindfulness teaches, you will often find that you can connect with a deeper sense of knowing that can be found in your body. It's hard to put this into words – but the more you practise this, the more you'll get a sense of it. You'll start to notice that you make wise decisions based more on whether something *feels* right in the body, rather than just what logic might dictate. Each person's body cues are different – but some signs of good decisions might include relaxation, a sense of groundedness and contentment in your belly, or a warm glow in your heart area. And signs of an unwise decision could include tension, shallow breathing, a knot in the stomach or a tight chest.

- **Choosing a good time to reflect**. Of course, eventually, you may feel you need to make your mind up about what to do. If so, it's best if you can set aside some time in advance when you can reflect – a time when you know you won't be disturbed and that you can give the matter your full attention. You may want to do some simple meditation before you reflect – and to notice some cues in your body as described above. You may also want to set yourself a deadline by when you will make your decision. If you find that you're not ready to do this when it comes to that time, you can consciously choose to come back to it another time. The key here is about being fully aware of what you are doing, and ring-fencing your deliberation time so that it doesn't interfere with the rest of your life.

Emotional intelligence

'Emotional intelligence' is about being able to recognise a full range of emotions in yourself and in other people. Then it's about working more effectively with this information to increase your wellbeing, to be more effective in what you put your mind to, and to build better relationships with others. You may be pleased to hear that the best training for developing emotional intelligence is mindfulness. That's because being mindful means being more aware of what is going on in your experience, *including your emotions*. It also means learning better strategies to *be with* difficult emotions, and allowing them to come and go rather than reacting automatically to them. There are two ways that enhanced emotional intelligence can play out in your life:

1) Self-awareness, self-esteem and confidence
As you really get to know yourself better, through mindfulness practice, you are more likely to be honest and balanced with yourself about both your positive qualities, and aspects of yourself that are harder to deal with. You can see yourself 'in the round' – fairly, realistically and kindly. This can lead you to feeling much clearer about your priorities and goals in life, based on an accurate self-assessment. And this is the basis for a steady self-confidence – a well-founded, truthful view of your abilities and worth.

For example, let's imagine someone who recognises that some of their positive qualities include generosity, good humour and courage. If they are able to acknowledge these fully – then they can enjoy and make best use of them. They will also probably be more able to see clearly other aspects of themselves that cause difficulties. In this case, perhaps this person might recognise that they sometimes have a short temper and rush to unhelpful conclusions. With this kind of self-awareness, they're more able to see that these aspects are not the whole of who they are. That can mean they are better placed to address these parts of themselves – and to learn ways to mitigate their effects.

2) Empathy, communication and kindness

It's well known that humans are a social species – needing good relationships with others for life to flourish. And to enhance your relationships it's very helpful to be able to 'read' and appreciate what is going on for other people emotionally. This is what is meant by 'empathy': the ability to imagine the world from another person's perspective. What's heartening to know is that humans have evolved to be empathic. Studies of the brain have revealed the presence of 'mirror neurons' – they fire off both when you do something and when you watch someone else do it. It's as if the brain was designed with other people in mind. The best training to enhance empathy is mindfulness. That's because it's so closely related to self-awareness, which is what you've been training to develop. In fact, the brain uses the same part (the insula) to perform both functions.

As a result, in one sense, to develop empathy all you need to do is carry on with your mindfulness training. As you get more familiar with your own emotions, and learn how to be with them more effectively, you will naturally become more empathic. And with empathy naturally comes the ability to choose wise responses when you are communicating with others: leading to better relationships with friends, family, colleagues, and even complete strangers.

That said, it's possible to take empathy to a higher level by consciously following the ABC mindfulness model when interacting with other people. Here's an example. Imagine you turn up late to a meeting with a friend or colleague, due to transport problems. As soon as you see your friend/colleague, before you have a chance to say anything, they tell you that they've been waiting ages and are really annoyed. This is how the ABC mindfulness approach might help you deal with this situation:

Awareness. As your friend/colleague tells you off, you can notice any responses in your body sensations and thoughts. You might notice that feelings of tightness in your chest, and thoughts like 'It's not fair, it wasn't my fault,' or 'You're so mean' or 'I'm useless.' This whole process of noticing what's going on inside you only need take a split second. The key thing is just remembering to notice.

Being with: This is really just an extension of the first stage of Awareness, but taken deeper. In particular, it's about noticing what automatic response you would normally reach for. In this case, it might include snapping back at the other person, or at the other end of the spectrum, making an excessive apology. The key thing is just to notice these urges to act and the 'reflex feelings' *in your body*, without yet choosing to do anything. This self-guided process still only need take a split second.

Choosing a wise response: Having taken a moment to notice what automatic reactions are going on, you can then tune in to what's *really* going on in the situation. A good way to do this is to ask yourself what both you and the other person are *feeling*, and also why you're feeling these things. In other words, what basic human *need* are you and they trying to get met?

In this example, you might notice that you are feeling sad or angry that your friend/colleague appears to be annoyed. That's because you have a need to be treated with respect and fairness. Or you might be feeling guilty – and that's because you have a need to treat others the same way. And you may also notice that all the same things are true of your friend and colleague – and that this explains why they seem to be annoyed. You might also recognise that they are someone who values punctuality highly.

When you can fully acknowledge the presence of these feelings and the causes of them in both yourself and the other person, you'll usually find yourself better placed to say something that diffuses the situation.

The wisest response is usually when you can be *assertive* about your own feelings and needs, while also *understanding* the other person's feelings and needs. Being assertive is like the middle way between two unhelpful extremes – being aggressive and being passive. So you might say something along the lines of 'I'm sorry to have kept you waiting. I can understand that this must have been very frustrating for you, as I know your time is precious. I fully intended to get here on time, but got delayed on transport. It was frustrating for me as well, as I don't like keeping people waiting.' Of course, it may not come out quite as neatly and precisely as that! But it's about the essence of the communication – allowing it to take into full consideration the feelings and needs of both you and the other person.

Acting kindly

When you develop mindfulness you are also developing your natural human capacity for kindness and compassion. Mindfulness training is not only about you and how you are: it is also about becoming more tuned in to your environment and the other people in it. You may have already noticed this in your experience. The audio meditations for both this chapter and the previous one deliberately bring in the concept of connecting with the quality of kindness towards yourself and others. This isn't about being 'nice' for its own sake. Rather it's about recognising the simple truth that your wellbeing depends on good relationships with others. And so being kind is like 'enlightened self-interest' – human beings tend to feel better in themselves when they are able to care about others' wellbeing.

You can take this kindness practice out into your everyday life by way of a very simple but powerful technique. Each time you meet someone – regardless of who they are – in your mind's eye, simply wish them well. If that's hard to do, perhaps remind yourself that, just like you, they are prone to the same fundamental struggles common to all humans, and that they want to be happy. This doesn't mean you have to like or approve of everyone – that's different from wishing them well. If this sounds challenging, then perhaps just remain open to what happens as you start practising it.

Mindfulness and other people

Self-care: developing your own 'manual' for your life

The self-awareness that mindfulness enables can lead to a clearer understanding of what activities and pursuits promote your general wellbeing and sense of fulfilment. As you will probably know from your experience, some activities nourish you and make you feel alive ('up' activities); others tire you out and make you feel low ('down' activities). Of course which activities are 'up' ones will differ for each person. But generally speaking, most are of two main types:

- *Mastery*: this includes both skills that you learn and develop (e.g. a musical instrument, a sport, a new language, a piece of computer software, etc.); also, more basic things that you need to do to make life organised and run smoothly, e.g. cleaning, tidying up, planning the week ahead, etc. These are best broken down into small chunks. And it's really good to congratulate and reward yourself when you've achieved them.

- *Pleasure*: things that you really enjoy doing, e.g. taking a long bath, eating your favourite food, going for a walk, seeing a friend, watching a good film, listening to music, etc.

You may have noticed that when you get very busy you may tend to give up the things that are actually nourishing, but may seem less 'urgent'. Rather than providing extra energy, this tends to be depleting, as the source of energy is cut off. Then with less energy, you are likely to give up even more nourishing activities – again due to a mistaken belief that you just need to cut out anything that's not essential. This cycle can continue to the point of exhaustion.

That's why, if you want to feel really well and happy in yourself, it's helpful if you can choose to spend more time doing 'up' activities and less time doing 'down' activities. Of course, the circumstances of your life may limit what can and can't be changed. But it's worth just checking in with yourself what realistic changes you could make to your everyday life. Often the smallest change can lead to noticeable positive results, which can then provide motivation to make more changes.

Motivation and flow

By getting to know and appreciate yourself more deeply through mindfulness – particularly your guiding values and the activities that promote your wellbeing – you are more likely to find the energy and determination to live according to those values. This can become the source of ongoing motivation. It can propel you towards concerted, determined action in a direction that feels right to you. When this happens, there are no such things as 'mistakes' or 'failures' – just opportunities to learn and adapt along the way.

When you approach life in this way, you are more likely to choose activities that stretch and challenge you just enough for you to be able to engage with them, without being overwhelmed by them. When this happens you can enter a state of 'flow' – when you are completely involved in the activity and it's inherently rewarding and enjoyable. You can probably think of moments of such 'flow' in your life – for example, when you were totally absorbed in a book, or in a fascinating conversation, or learning a new skill.

Flow and the 'stress curve'

Another way to understand 'flow' or motivation is through the 'stress curve' shown below. Stress is usually considered to be a bad thing, but in fact there is such a thing as 'good stress' (eustress). You need just the right amount of 'stress' to perform at your best – and when this happens it can feel like you are in a state of flow, and you naturally feel motivated, too. This is like the 'zone of optimal performance'. If there's too little or too much stress, you underperform. The key to peak performance is to know when there's just the right amount of stress.

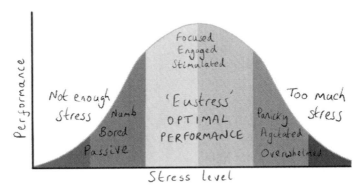

Stress curve showing the 'zone of optimal performance'

Commitment

Sometimes it might seem like this desirable state of flow is completely out of reach. You may feel very unmotivated at times – even low and despondent. This is often particularly the case if you experience some kind of 'setback', or you find yourself breaking some commitment you might have made to yourself or others. At these times, there's a simple mindfulness-based approach you might find helpful to re-establish a sense of motivation and determination. Here's an example.

Imagine you want to get fitter by doing more exercise. Recently you haven't been doing any exercise at all. You decide that you're going to exercise every day for at least 30 minutes. You set a start date for the new regime. When you get to the end of the first week, you realise you've only exercised once.

1. Awareness: Notice how you are feeling in your mind and body. What are you thinking and feeling? In this case, you might notice that you are feeling disappointed in yourself –

maybe sad, or even a bit angry. Thoughts that might accompany these feelings could include: 'I'm useless, I can't even do this simple thing' or 'I've got no discipline, so there's no point even trying.'

2. Objective assessment and learning: Are the thoughts and feelings you are having in line with the reality of the situation? Is there a way of describing it that is true without being a harsh judgement on yourself? What can you learn from what's happened that is genuinely helpful to take into the future? In this example, you might recall that you do actually have quite good discipline and are not 'useless', because you taught yourself a new skill recently and that required regular practice (perhaps that's doing mindfulness practice!). You might also recognise that you have actually started to do some exercise, which is better than before, when you were doing none. You might also realise that your original commitment to exercise every day was too ambitious, considering you weren't doing any before.

3. Starting afresh: Based on the above, what new commitment do you want to make that, right now, you believe is both positive and realistic? In this example you might want to renew your overall commitment to getting fitter, and decide that exercising three days a week is a more likely and possible way to achieve this, based on what you've learned.

Realistic optimism

Making wise choices in the ways described above can also lead to a subtle shift towards a more optimistic outlook on life. To understand this, it's worth noticing how the human mind has evolved to think rather negatively. There are two reasons for this. First, the constant danger for early humans meant that the mind's primary programming was all about 'avoiding getting killed'. Secondly, the need to belong to a group (in order to survive) led to a strong tendency for people to make comparisons with others within their social group to check that they 'fit in'. And unfortunately, it's easy to come off feeling second best (e.g. 'I am not as good as them').

Taken together these are a strong recipe for pessimism. By training in mindfulness you can learn to let go of this evolutionary tendency – simply by noticing that it's there and creating more 'distance' from it. And by living according to your values and finding the motivation to act consistently in that direction, you can set up a virtuous circle in your life. The positive changes you notice give you yet more energy to get things done. When this happens, you may notice that optimism naturally comes about.

However, it's also possible to consciously train in the practice of 'optimism' – as a natural extension of mindfulness training. Let's look at this through an example:

You apply for a job you'd love to do. You get invited to an interview. You go to the interview, and think it's gone really well, but then find out you didn't get the job. Later you get feedback saying that they were extremely impressed with your skills, experience and attitude; you were a very strong candidate for the job, and it was a tough call to choose the most appropriate person to offer the job.

In this scenario, you may end up feeling really downhearted about not getting the job, and take it to mean all sorts of awful things about you and your future. However, taking a realistically optimistic approach, you could instead follow a different thinking and feeling process:

Step 1. Being realistic and objective: Just notice and describe to yourself what's actually happened. In this example, that is simply that you didn't get the job you wanted, but that they gave you very good feedback.

Step 2. Giving yourself permission to feel whatever emotion arises: In this example, most people will feel sad or disappointed. It's important to allow yourself to feel this, while not getting stuck in it or buying into difficult thoughts that may accompany it (e.g. 'I'm not good enough to get a decent job').

Step 3. Changing your automatic approach to success and failure: With a success, you can take conscious note of it and accept the credit for it. In this example, although you did not achieve the ultimate 'success' of getting the job, you did succeed in being considered worthy of very positive feedback. You can allow yourself to enjoy this feedback, without pretending to yourself that you're not disappointed not to have got the job. And with failure, you can focus on realistic evidence that it's only temporary, and that it's in the context of lots of other successes in your life. In this case, you can isolate the failure simply to the fact that you did not get this particular job, rather than it being a major failing in you. And you can take genuine heart in the positive feedback, and allow it to be evidence that you have what it takes to get a different job that you will feel equally excited about.

Whoever you are and whatever you've done in life, this kind of realistic optimism is always possible. And these steps, when practised often enough, can become a new mental habit of optimism that can balance out a strong negative bias.

Gratitude and happiness

Just as it's possible to train in optimism, so too it's possible to learn how to be happier. Happiness can seem elusive – and research shows that everyone tends to have their own set-point of happiness that they return to, regardless of what happens. In fact, it's been shown that the causes of happiness can be divided up as follows:

- 50% = Genetic inheritance
- 10% = External circumstance (education level, income, etc.)
- 40% = Day-to-day behaviour and thinking

It's in the last of these that mindfulness training can make a significant difference. Research has shown that one of the best ways to cultivate happiness is to develop a more 'appreciative' awareness of what's going on around us. As seen already, the human mind has evolved to have a negative bias – and it tends to filter out much of the good 'stuff' that happens. When you consciously choose to notice this good stuff more, it can affect the way you think and behave – and you create a new positive mental habit.

A good way to develop this habit is to write down, every day, three things you're grateful for, or things that other people have done for you that have benefited you. These don't all have to be hugely significant events – they can also be day-to-day things that in hindsight you notice gave you pleasure or made life easier for you. For example, it could be a smile and kind word a friend or stranger gave you, a tasty meal you ate, a bird singing in a tree, a TV programme that made you laugh.

To take this 'gratitude' practice to the next level, it can be really helpful not only to write down what you're grateful for, but also to share it with others. And if you're grateful to others for something they've done – you could express your appreciation to them. When you verbalise your gratitude, you amplify it and feel it more deeply within you. Many people find that the 'feeling' of gratitude is just inherently pleasurable.

A gentle word of warning: don't try too hard

This chapter has suggested a range of mindfulness-based 'techniques' that you can use to develop your ability to make choices and decisions that enhance the quality of your life and the lives of those around you. You are encouraged to see what happens if you make a conscious effort to put them into practice. At the same time, it's important not to set your expectations too high, or feel that you have failed if something doesn't seem to be working. Everyone is different, and so some things will work for some people and not for others, or at a different pace. So try to approach it all lightly, with an attitude of curiosity and patience.

In other words, don't try too hard. When embarking on a process of personal development like this, it's always good to try and get a balance between two things: on the one hand, making a really concerted effort to bring about change; on the other hand, simply accepting things as they are. Everyone needs both approaches at different times and to different degrees. It's no coincidence that this is exactly the same approach that you are encouraged to take in meditation – getting a balance between effort and relaxation, and knowing when you need more of one or the other.

Wise choices meditation

The 'wise choices' audio guided meditation will take you through the stages to practise the essence of what's been covered in this chapter. Here is a brief overview of what happens in the meditation:

Stage 1: Awareness of your body and breath (as in the 'waking up to yourself' meditation).

Stage 2: Connecting with your strength and kindness. Taking your attention into the areas around your belly (for strength) and your heart (for kindness), and allowing these natural qualities to be felt, even if only dimly (as in the 'acceptance' meditation).

Stage 3: Bringing to mind some issue in your life that is in some way difficult for you. Noticing what comes up as a result – particularly sensations in your body that call for your attention. Turning towards sensations in the body. Noticing particularly if there are strong sensations – pleasant or unpleasant – and if there is an urge to push them away or hold on to them. Exploring the sensations, using your imagination and your breath to help you stay with them. Saying to yourself: *'It's OK – whatever it is, it's OK. Let me feel it.'*

Stage 4: Opening up wise choices – reflecting on how you could approach this difficulty in a way that's different from your habitual ways.

Using the three-step breathing space to practise wise choices

You can use the three-step breathing space – already introduced in the previous two chapters – to practise making wise choices as and when you need to. You follow the same steps as before, but with an emphasis on allowing new perspectives and choices to come into your awareness in the last stage:

1. *Awareness*: Adopting a posture that is both relaxed and alert. Taking a few slightly deeper breaths, and as you breathe in, imagining the breath moving up and giving your back and neck an uplift. As you breathe out, imagining it travelling down your front. Now tuning in to yourself. Get an overall sense of your experience right now. What am I thinking? What mood am I in? What can I feel in my body?

2. *Gathering*: Bring the focus of your awareness onto your breathing.

3. *Expanding*: Broadening out your awareness to include your whole body and facial expression. Bring to mind whatever issue is going on for you that you want to resolve. Gently asking yourself, what do I know deep down would be a wise response here? What would really be in my best interests? And those of other people?

Short summary of this chapter

By learning the two first core skills of Awareness and Being with experience, you already have all you need to make naturally wise choices in your life. That's because you can create a gap between an initial event and your next move, and choose a wise response. This goes for both the everyday events and the big decisions in your life. There are various aspects of life where you can enhance your ability to make wise choices:

Connecting with your values and purpose

Self-awareness includes identifying your core values - the guiding principles about what you want to stand for. Your choices in life are more likely to be wise if they are in accordance with these values. It's worth spending some time reflecting on your core values – and finding your top ten.

Clearer thinking and better planning

Mindfulness promotes a better quality of thinking processes than run-of-the-mill automatic thinking. This leads to better planning, organisational and decision-making skills. It's due to your ability to pay attention to the detail while also seeing the big picture. You train this skill in meditation by being able to switch between a narrow focus (e.g. just your left big toe) and a broader awareness (your whole body).

Emotional intelligence

Emotional intelligence is about being able to recognise emotions in yourself and other people, and working more effectively with this information to increase your wellbeing, to be more effective, and to build better relationships with others. Mindfulness is the best training for it because it teaches you how to be aware of and 'hold' all your experience, including your emotions.

1) Self-awareness, self-esteem and confidence
As you get to know yourself better, you can be more honest and balanced about your strengths and weaknesses. This can lead to feeling clearer about your priorities and goals in life, which is the basis for a realistic self-confidence.

2) Empathy, communication and kindness
'Empathy' is the ability to imagine the world from another

person's perspective — a vital skill in forming good relationships. It's possible to consciously enhance empathy by using the same ABC of mindfulness applied to communication and relationships with other people:

A. _Awareness_: of your thoughts, emotions and body sensations, when you are communicating with someone

B. _Being with_: noticing any automatic reactions and choosing to stay with them for a moment before acting

C. _Choosing a wise response_: tuning in to what's _really_ going on in the situation by considering what both you and the other person are _feeling_, and what your _needs_ are. This can help you choose a wise response — which is usually when you can be _assertive_ about your own feelings and needs, while also being _understanding and kind_ about the other person's feelings and needs.

Acting kindly

Developing empathy means you also develop your natural human capacity for kindness and compassion. This isn't about being 'nice' for its own sake. It's about recognising that your wellbeing depends on good relationships with others. You can take this kindness practice out into your everyday life: each time you meet someone — in your mind's eye — simply wish them well. This doesn't mean you have to like or approve of everyone — but you can still wish them well.

Self-care: developing your own 'manual' for your life

Self-awareness also includes understanding what activities and pursuits promote your general wellbeing and sense of fulfilment. Some activities tend to nourish you and make you feel alive ('up' activities); others are more likely to tire you out and make you feel low ('down'). Most 'up' activities are of two main types:

- *Mastery*: skills that you learn; basic things that you need to do to make life organised and run smoothly.

- *Pleasure*: things that you really enjoy doing, e.g. taking a long bath, eating your favourite food, going for a walk, seeing a friend, watching a good film, listening to music, etc. When people are very busy they tend to give up nourishing activities that seem less 'urgent'. This tends to deplete energy rather than boost it. With less energy they then cut off even more nourishing activities – setting up a vicious cycle leading to exhaustion. To counteract this, it's good to choose to spend more time on 'up' activities and less time on 'down' ones.

Commitment

If you have a setback in life, mindfulness can help you recover. The key is to check if your thoughts and feelings are in line with reality – and to find a different way of describing things that's true without being harsh. Then you can start afresh, and make a new commitment that's positive while also being realistic.

Realistic optimism

You can consciously enhance 'optimism' in three steps:

1. Be realistic and objective in every situation – just notice and describe what's actually happened.

2. Give yourself permission to feel whatever emotion arises in any given situation.

3. Change your automatic approach to success and failure. Take conscious note of successes and accept the credit for them. With failures, focus on realistic evidence that they are only temporary, and are in the context of lots of other successes in your life.

Gratitude and happiness

Research shows that one of the biggest factors for happiness is day-to-day behaviour and thinking. Mindfulness has a role here – so that you can actually train in happiness. A good way to do this is to develop your 'appreciative' awareness by noting down frequently things you're grateful for. Sharing this with others helps embed this skill further.

Home practice before the next chapter

To stream or download the audio guided meditations listed below, go to: risingminds.org.uk/mindfulness

1. Alternate each day between these two practices:
- **'Wise choices' meditation** – follow the instructions on the audio meditation.
- **'Movement meditation'** – follow the audio instructions.

2. Three-step breathing space: Practise this as a way to find a wise choice quickly in a situation: either on your own, or listening to the audio.

3. Mindful communication: When you're in communication with someone else, see if you can be more aware of your own feelings and needs, and sense what theirs are, too.

4. Do something different: Strike up a conversation with someone you don't know.

Journaling: In your journal jot down some notes about which 'up' activities you could do more of, and which 'down' activities you could do less of.

Chapter 6
Taking mindfulness into your future

You've arrived at the final chapter. At the risk of being clichéd, this ending is also a beginning. It's the beginning of a new phase in your life, where you have the opportunity to put the principles and practices of mindfulness fully into practice in your own life. This final chapter looks at some ways to help you keep your mindfulness practice alive, and also to make it your own — so that it works for you and the circumstances of your life. In doing so, hopefully you will feel motivated to keep using the basic tools taught here, and then to refine them in a way that supports your wellbeing and effectiveness in every area of your life.

Keeping mindfulness alive

Hopefully you're discovering that mindfulness is a skill that not only helps you deal more effectively with problems and difficult emotions, but also that simply makes life richer and more fulfilling. Like any skill, regular practice helps keep it fresh and potent. So, if you feel like you've gained a lot from this programme, perhaps you'll want to make a commitment to yourself to keep using the tools you've learned. You may find it helpful to think of some positive motivations now that you could look back on in future times of difficulty. What could you remind yourself of in the future that will help you remember to use your new skills?

There are two main ways in which you can keep your mindfulness practice alive: 1) in formal meditation; 2) outside of meditation. There will be more about meditation at the end of this chapter. As for what you can do throughout your day, many people find it helpful to make a few simple mindful activities a regular part of their daily routine. These don't need to take any extra time, but they can really help you stay more present and to make wise choices, from moment to moment. It's about weaving mindfulness into the fabric of your day. Here are a few suggestions:

- When you wake, and before you go to sleep, observe five mindful breaths.
- When you need to, take a few mindful breaths to ground yourself and to help you come back into awareness of the present moment.
- Mindful eating – feel the food's nourishment, taste and smell it.
- Bring simple mindful awareness to routine physical activities like preparing food, washing up, driving, walking, etc.
- Use the three-step breathing space – which can be done in as little as one minute.
- Use otherwise 'dead' time as an opportunity for mindfulness practice, particularly when you have no choice but to wait for something – for example, when queuing, waiting at the traffic lights, or waiting for a train or bus.

There are in fact countless opportunities to practise mindfulness. It doesn't need to be some 'extra' thing you add to your to do list. Instead you can bring the essence of mindful attention to whatever you are doing, at any time. The more you can do this, the more you will find that a mindful approach becomes second nature to you.

Everyday mindfulness

Making it your own

On this programme you have learned a range of techniques for developing a mindful approach to life. They are well tried and tested techniques – and have been shown in clinical research to be highly effective in enhancing wellbeing and creative thinking. However, it's vital to stress that for mindfulness to have the biggest possible impact on your life it needs to feel like it's *your own* practice. Indeed, the ultimate aim of mindfulness is to empower you to lead your life in a way that feels authentic and meaningful *to you* – rather than according to some preconceived idea about how you should live. So a fully mindful life means finding out what really matters to you and then following that thread. It's about being autonomous and independent – being the master of your life. It's about unleashing your innate creativity so that you can respond positively to life with full awareness.

All this being so, you are encouraged to use the techniques taught here as a springboard from which you can develop your own unique ways of practising mindfulness. So as you carry on practising, remain open to which particular techniques work for you, and feel free to adapt them. That could mean altering the stages of a meditation; coming up with your own definition of mindfulness; or discovering which activities particularly promote mindfulness for you. For mindfulness to work for you, it needs to feel like a constantly evolving approach to your particular personality and life circumstances. It needs to feel alive and creative. So enjoy making it your own.

Practising with other people

While it's vital to make mindfulness your own, many people also find that to keep it going it's helpful to practise alongside other people or to get ongoing support. The same goes for many other life pursuits – like playing an instrument or a sport, or learning a new skill. Practising mindfulness with others can help you keep up motivation, as well as learning from each other. So, it can be worth finding or creating a meditation group that meets regularly to practise together and share notes about how it's going. You could find a meditation group that meets regularly in your local area – as mindfulness becomes more popular, there are more and more such groups around. An internet search on 'meditation groups + your local area' should throw up some options. You could also do more formal training at the wide range of public centres offering mindfulness courses – again, just do an internet search.

Life manual

In the previous chapter you were invited to spend a bit of time reflecting and writing about 'up' activities (ones that make you feel alive and well) and 'down' activities (ones that make you feel tired or low). It could be really helpful to keep reflecting and writing about this over the next few weeks and months. Don't think of it as a chore – just keep the question floating around your mind and jot down anything as it comes in a little notebook. Keep the notebook with you at all times. It's like the first draft of the most important book you'll ever read: your guide for yourself on how to live your best life. It's your life manual. Every now and then you might want to flick through it and see what wisdom you've come up with for yourself. Maybe eventually you could write it all down in some kind of logical order. That's entirely up to you: do whatever is most helpful for you and your life.

Taking meditation forward

Selecting a meditation for each occasion

The guided audio meditations on this programme have been taking you through a natural sequence of mindfulness training following the ABC of mindfulness. The audio meditations are 'cumulative' – i.e. as they progress, each includes the stages from the previous one.

A: Awareness of your experience – your body sensations, thoughts and emotions. In doing this, you train your attention-paying 'muscles'. (The 'waking up to yourself' meditation)

B: Being with your experience – learning to turn towards sensations, thoughts and emotions, to investigate them with openness and patience. In doing this, you train your ability to understand and process your experience more, so that autopilot isn't always in the driving seat. (The 'working with your thoughts' meditation and then the 'acceptance' meditation)

C: Choosing wise responses – having allowed yourself to be with your experience, you remain open to new perspectives and choices. In doing this you train your ability to respond more creatively, which enhances your wellbeing and effectiveness. (The 'wise choices' meditation)

You may find that you want to keep listening to some or all of the guided audio meditations to help you embed this natural sequence in your mind. Each meditation might be most useful on different occasions:

- *'Waking up to yourself' meditation and/or 'movement meditation'*: if you get a sense that you need just to re-establish some basic awareness.

- *'Working with your thoughts' meditation*: if you notice that you're caught up in a lot of negative thoughts.

- *'Acceptance' meditation*: if you're aware that you're finding it difficult to stay with something difficult.

- *'Wise choices' meditation*: if there's a decision you need to make or a particular issue that you need to get some fresh perspectives on.

As you hone your mindfulness skills and get more familiar with the different techniques and stages, you'll get more of an intuitive sense about which meditation is most appropriate at different times. You may also find after a while that you don't want to listen to the audio guided versions any more. Instead you could just set a timer for however long you want to meditate and follow the steps in your own mind in silence.

Advanced meditation – 'open awareness'

As you mature with mindfulness, you might also like to experiment with a more advanced approach called 'open awareness'. In this approach, you start with the A of the ABC – grounding yourself in awareness of your breath and body. Then in the latter stage of the meditation, you enter into a more fluid mix of both the B and the C – Being with, and Choosing wise responses. You can allow yourself to stand back a bit from your experience and simply observe what particularly calls for your attention – be that a thought, a memory, an image, a body sensation or an emotion. Whatever comes up for you, you can choose to make this the focus of the meditation. In your mind's eye, you can turn towards it, and see how you're relating to it. If you're pushing it away or holding on to it somehow, can you relax a bit around it, and give it some more space? What might it be trying to communicate to you, perhaps in relation to some current issue in your life? Then, when it's no longer calling for your attention, or you reach some kind of clarity or resolution on that issue, you can return to awareness of the body/breath – until the next significant thing comes into your awareness. In taking this approach, you are flexing two vital complementary aspects of mindfulness: focused awareness (depth) and broad awareness (breadth).

The beauty of this approach to mindfulness is that it reinforces the essential point that there's nothing that you either should or shouldn't be experiencing. Anything that comes up is fine and worthy of attention. It also applies to many common difficulties that people experience in meditation (and outside meditation!) including: drowsiness, low concentration, boredom, anxiety, fear, restlessness, etc. Rather than making them into 'problems' that should be avoided or fought off, instead you simply allow yourself to be aware of what they feel like in your body, and how you are relating to them. By doing this, you are more likely to find out something interesting about yourself and your usual patterns of thoughts and feelings.

You may find it hard to adopt this approach to meditation at first, as it might feel like there are so many competing thoughts, feelings and emotions coming and going rapidly – all vying for your attention. If so, it might be that you need to return to a more focused awareness of your body and breath to help ground you a bit more. Experiment with it, and see what you learn in the process.

Short summary of this chapter

Mindfulness is a skill, and like any skill, regular practice helps keep it fresh and potent. To keep your mindfulness practice alive, you can make a few simple mindful activities a regular part of your daily routine. These don't need to take any extra time, but they can really help you stay more present and to make wise choices, from moment to moment. For example:

- When you wake, and before you go to sleep, observe five mindful breaths.
- Take a few mindful breaths when you need to.
- Mindful eating – feel the food's nourishment, taste and smell it.

- Bring simple mindful awareness to routine physical activities.
- Use the three-step breathing space – in as little as one minute.
- Practise mindfulness in 'dead' time – e.g. when queuing, or waiting for a train or bus, etc.

Making it your own

The ultimate aim of mindfulness is for you to lead your life in a way that feels right and meaningful *to you* – rather than according to some preconceived idea about how you should live. So as you carry on practising, remain open to which particular techniques work for you, and feel free to adapt them. It needs to feel alive and creative. So enjoy making it your own.

Practising with other people

Practising mindfulness alongside other people can help you keep up motivation – and you can learn from each other. You could do that with a group of people you already know or join a meditation group in your area. Or you could do more formal training at a public centre. Some internet research should throw up some options in your local area.

Life manual

It could be really helpful to keep reflecting and writing about what are 'up' and 'down' activities for you. Jot down thoughts in a notebook. This is like your 'life manual' – your guide for yourself on how best to live your life. Eventually you could write it all down in some kind of logical order if that's helpful.

Selecting a meditation for each occasion

You may find that you want to keep listening to the guided audio meditations, and to choose which one to listen to at different times:

- *'Waking up to yourself' meditation and/or 'movement meditation'*: if you get a sense that you need just to re-establish some basic awareness.
- *'Working with your thoughts' meditation*: if you notice that you're caught up in a lot of negative thoughts.
- *'Acceptance' meditation*: if you're aware that you're finding it difficult to stay with something difficult.
- *'Wise choices' meditation*: if there's a particular issue that's troubling you that you need to get some fresh perspectives on.
- *Open awareness meditation (see below)* – when you are feeling more confident and experienced in mindfulness, and want to deepen your levels of awareness.

After a while you may not want to listen to the audio versions. Instead you could just set a timer for however long you want to meditate, and follow the steps in your own mind in silence.

Advanced meditation – 'open awareness'

As you mature with mindfulness, a more advanced approach you might try is called 'open awareness'. This starts with grounding yourself in awareness of your breath and body. Then for the rest of the meditation, you stand back from your experience and simply observe what particularly calls for your attention – thoughts, memories, images, body sensations or emotions. Whatever comes up, make this the focus of the meditation. Turn towards it and give it more space. See what it might be trying to communicate to you. Then, when it's no longer calling for your attention, return to awareness of the body/breath – until the next significant thing comes into your awareness.

Home practice from now on ... and indefinitely!

To stream or download the audio guided meditations, go to: risingminds.org.uk/mindfulness

1. Meditation – work with a combination of any of the main meditations – either with or without the audio guided versions.

2. Daily mindfulness – refer to the suggestions above.

3. Getting to know yourself better – keep writing your 'life manual', as described above.

4. Keep doing something different – use your imagination!

Short summary of the whole book

What's the point of mindfulness?

There are inevitable problems in life – the body experiences pain; the mind experiences difficult emotions because humans don't always get what they want or avoid what they don't want. But the bigger problem comes from the mind's 'autopilot' response to try to fix things instantly. This 'doing' or 'avoidance' mode evolved in early humans when they needed to find a quick solution to avoid danger. Today it's still useful in getting through life, as it allows you to get stuff done without needing to work out how each time. But it's closely linked with the fight/flight/freeze response, which wards off threats by automatically sending energy to the muscles and releasing stress hormones. In the process there's less energy available for essential body maintenance and higher brain functioning. So if autopilot causes this stress response to kick in too often, it's bad not only for physical health but also for mental health – as you can't process emotions properly or think clearly. And when autopilot fails to fix things, the problem can seem even worse as you may be left feeling frustrated or disheartened – leading into a destructive cycle of negative thinking and emotions.

How mindfulness works

Instead of using the 'doing' mode of autopilot, you can use a 'being' mode to resolve many problems and emotions more effectively. This being mode approaches things with gentle, interested curiosity, rather than trying to solve them instantly. It gives them space to be as they are. It's possible to train yourself to develop this mode of mind. This is what mindfulness training does: by learning to *pay attention, on purpose, in the present moment, without judgement. Or simply noticing what you notice*.

The ABC of Mindfulness

Awareness

Noticing with kindness and patience what is happening in your experience in your mind and body *in this moment*. Not trying to relax or to clear the mind of thoughts or feelings – just noticing them come and go.

Being with your experience

a. Working with your thoughts: Your autopilot mind always wants to make sense of things, which then creates a whole set of patterns and rules. This is where habitual thoughts come from, and they colour your view of the world: what you make of an event determines how you feel (Situation + Interpretation → Emotion). However, your thoughts are not facts – they are just patterns of your mind. Mindfulness of thoughts means noticing your most common thoughts and where they tend to lead you. Step outside them a bit and watch them come and go, like watching clouds passing across the sky. If the thought is very persistent, check if it fits with reality – and then refine it.

b. Acceptance: Autopilot tries to push away difficult emotions or problems. Instead, you can practise allowing yourself to turn towards and feel fully all your emotions and sensations. Give them space and explore them with curiosity, like a scientist examining a specimen. Accept them as they are, and then they are less likely to have such a hold over you – as they will pass in time. Say to yourself: *'It's OK – whatever it is, it's OK. Let me feel it.'* This doesn't mean giving in to them. Rather it means trusting that they want to be felt and carry useful information for you about what's really going on. As you practise acceptance, you'll get to know more which things you can change and which things you can't.

Choosing wise responses

Having given yourself more time and space to notice and accept your experience, you can allow wise responses to emerge naturally. This is about *responding* wisely instead of *reacting* automatically. You can consciously develop this ability by:

- *connecting with your values and purpose*: what really matters to you and how does that affect you right now?
- *being honest with yourself*: what's actually going on in this situation and what's in your power to change?
- *developing empathy*: becoming aware of what's going on for others, communicating kindly while assertively
- *doing more stuff that makes you feel good:* particularly things that give you a sense of mastery or pleasure
- *doing less stuff that makes you feel drained*
- *bouncing back from setbacks*: if something goes wrong, instead of giving yourself a hard time, give yourself honest feedback about what you could do differently next time, and make a new commitment for future action
- *practising optimism*: making a conscious effort to note your successes and appreciate your strengths/skills
- *practising gratitude*: appreciating what others have done for you (studies show this increases happiness).

Meditation

Set-up: Adopt a posture that is both relaxed and alert. Centre and ground yourself by taking a few slightly deeper breaths in and out of your belly. As you breathe in, imagine the breath moving up and giving your back and neck an uplift. As you breathe out, imagine it travelling down your front.

Approach: Be kind, gentle and patient with yourself. Get a balance between a focused, narrow awareness (concentration) and a broad, gentle awareness (mindfulness). Use your breath to practise switching between the two – focused awareness on the in-breath, broad awareness on the outbreath.

Audio meditations – which to use?

- *'Waking up to yourself'*: if you need to re-establish some basic awareness and calm.
- *'Working with your thoughts'*: if you're caught up in a lot of negative thoughts.
- *'Acceptance'*: if you're finding it difficult to stay with something difficult.
- *'Wise choices'*: if there's a decision to make or an issue you need clarity on.

Mini-meditations

Three-step breathing space

1. Awareness: Tune in to yourself and get a sense of your overall experience right now. What am I thinking? What mood am I in? What can I feel in my body?

2. Gathering: Bring the focus of your awareness onto your breathing.

3. Expanding: Broaden out your awareness to include your whole body and facial expression. Notice anything else coming to you through your senses: what can you hear, see, smell, taste and touch?

The mindful minute (or even only 30 seconds!)

1. Pause a moment. Notice your body and breath.
2. Notice two things you can see.
3. Notice two things you can hear.
4. Notice two things your body's touching.
5. Allow all of these to merge together.
6. Return to what you were doing.

Mindfulness on the move

- Notice your breathing.
- Mindful eating – feel the food's nourishment, taste and smell it.
- Notice physical sensations when doing routine activities (e.g. walking).
- Notice things around you – how things look, sound, smell, taste.
- Use 'dead' time to practise (e.g. queuing or waiting for a train).

Final word

If you can bring mindfulness into your life, hopefully you will feel happier, steadier and more fulfilled.

Printed in Great Britain
by Amazon